Experiment of Direct Democracy

Experiment of Direct Democracy

Gram Swaraj in Madhya Pradesh

YATINDRA SINGH SISODIA

RAWAT PUBLICATIONS

Jaipur • New Delhi • Bangalore • Mumbai • Hyderabad • Guwahati

ISBN 81-316-0097-1

The publication of this book was financially supported by ICSSR and the responsibility for the facts stated opinions expressed or conclusions reached, is entirely that of the author and that ICSSR accepts no responsibility for them.

ICSSR Consultant
Professor Arun Chaturvedi

Published by
Prem Rawat for **Rawat Publications**
Satyam Apts, Sector 3, Jawahar Nagar, Jaipur 302 004 (India)
Phone: 0141 265 1748 / 7006 Fax: 0141 265 1748
E-mail: info@rawatbooks.com
Website: www.rawatbooks.com

New Delhi Office
4858/24, Ansari Road, Daryaganj, New Delhi 110 002
Phone: 011 2326 3290

Also at Bangalore, Mumbai, Hyderabad and Guwahati

Typeset by Rawat Computers, Jaipur
Printed at Nice Printing Press, New Delhi

Contents

Preface

Village communities have been in existence in India for over centuries and panchayats have been an intimate part of the Indian culture. Panchayat system is one of the unique democratic institutions evolved in India by the country's own genius and ethos. After independence, efforts were made to create and strengthen the institutions of local self-governance but all in vain as the issue of people's participation at grassroots level was not taken into serious consideration. Sixty years of independence witnessed the multidimensional approach of various governments at Centre and in states for planned development of vast rural India. Despite plethora of schemes and massive investment in rural sector, the rural scenario remained grim with no infrastructure and basic amenities like road, water, electricity, school, hospital and opportunities for employment.

Panchayat Raj, in its rejuvenated form, seeks to achieve the objectives of democratic decentralisation to accelerate socio-economic development and usher in equity and social justice. The objectives of decentralisation are to execute and implement schemes and programmes to meet the local needs, to mobilise people, to channelise their energies towards socio-economic reconstruction and to involve them in all the activities of the communities through the new institutions. Its objectives include also to reduce the size of work of the higher level government and leaving the responsibility to the people to decide their destiny as per the new dispensation.

Madhya Pradesh is the first state in India, which not only prepared its state legislation in accordance with 73rd Constitution Amendment Act but also conducted election in May-June 1994. The state has responded with innovativeness and remarkable commitment to making the system sustainable and successful. Its effort to institutionalise the system is evident in the number of amendments that have been made to the State Panchayat Act as a dynamic response to the problems at the ground level. During the implementation of Panchayat Raj system, Madhya Pradesh has faced several opportunities and difficulties. The experience of the state is extremely rich and provides vital insights into the process of institutionalising Panchayat Raj.

The pioneering and innovative initiatives of the Madhya Pradesh government in strengthening and institutionalising decentralised rural self-governance in the post-73rd Amendment phase generated immense interest among the observers and experts who were keen to understand this significant change in the pattern of governance at the grassroots level. In the continuation of the process of strengthening institutional governance at local level, an innovation of Gram Swaraj system was introduced on 26 January 2001. In this context, it becomes imperative to go beyond the government's stated objectives, rules and regulations, Acts and claims of effective functioning of panchayats, and takes an objective look at the ground reality and also to understand and analyse the innovations made by the State Government through Gram Swaraj.

This study is an attempt to identify, document and comprehend the broad trends emanating from the field, based on the experience of three years' functioning of Gram Swaraj in Madhya Pradesh. Three years is a short span of time for the dust to settle from such radical changes. However, it is important to understand and analyse the process and direction of institutionalisation of the present system and its status in the initial phase (2001 to 2004), which would have a significant impact and critical lessons for charting out the future course of action for effective people-centric development and governance not only in the state but across the country.

This study is divided into seven chapters. First chapter provides detailed introduction of the study including the background of the Panchayat Raj in India. The second chapter consists of the constitutional framework of Panchayat Raj in Madhya Pradesh including the amendment package of Gram Swaraj. Third chapter elaborates study design. Fourth chapter documents the village situation and operationalisation of Gram Sabha. Ground realities of Panchayat Raj and Gram Swaraj are discussed in chapters five and six. Chapter five interprets the perceptions and attitudes of panchayat representatives whereas chapter six analyses the perceptions and attitudes of Gram Sabha members. Chapter seven concludes the study.

The present study was assigned by Indian Council of Social Science Research (ICSSR), New Delhi. I owe my gratitude to the ICSSR for commissioning the project. I further extend my indebtedness to ICSSR for generous grant, which has made this publication possible.

I would also like to express my deep sense of gratitude to Professor R.S. Gautam, President, Madhya Pradesh Institute of Social Science Research (MPISSR) for his sustained encouragement, valuable advice with appreciation and encouragement to work purposively.

I am deeply indebted to Professor B.R. Purohit for his special interest in the present study. His immense insight, continuing and sustained guidance have been of special help for me to complete this task. He took special pains to go through the first draft of the report and made many constructive suggestions which extensively helped me to finalise the report in the present form.

I would like to express my sincere thanks to Professor D.C. Sah, Director, MPISSR for extending valuable suggestions on various steps of the project.

I am thankful to my colleagues Shri L.P. Gautam, Dr. Sandeep Joshi, Dr. Ashish Bhatt, Dr. S.S. Chandel and Dr. Manu Gautam for their valuable suggestions and help extended during the entire period of this project.

My sincere thanks are due to my research team, specially Dr. Mahendra Singh Yadav, who worked with me in the entire course of this study. My thanks are due to all the respondents who spared their valuable time to answer our questions.

I wish to thank Shri Sudeep Mishra for presenting the report in present form.

I would like to express my personal thanks to my better half Mrs. Surya for her constant encouragement and support in my academic endeavours.

Finally, I must confess that I alone am responsible for the observations made and conclusions drawn in this study.

Yatindra Singh Sisodia

Glossary of Terms

Adhiniyam	Act
Adhyaksha	President
Adhosarovachna Samiti	Infrastructure Committee
Anganwadi	A centre, under a Government of India programme – Integrated Child Development Services (ICDS), where supplementary food is provided to pregnant women and infant children
Anna Kosh	A kind of store where people are supposed to deposit their extra grain that could be used by other persons on some terms and conditions
Bhawan	Building
Dalit	Scheduled Caste
Gram Kosh	Village account
Gram Panchayat	The lowest tier of the Panchayat Raj which is formed on the basis of population and consists of one or more than one revenue village. The population of a panchayat cannot be less than 1,000

Gram Raksha Samiti	Village Protection Committee
Gram Sabha	The assembly of the persons of a revenue village whose names are included in the voters list
Gram Swaraj	Village self rule
Gram Vikas Samiti	Village Development Committee
Janpad Panchayat	The second tier of the Panchayat Raj institutions, i.e., the council of the elected representatives at the block level
Kharanja	Stone/brick road
Krishi Samiti	Agriculture Committee
Kosh	Account
Kotwar/Chaukidar	The person who works as the guard of the village
Munadi	Public announcement
Nagad Kosh	Cash account
Nirman	Construction
Panch	The elected representative of a Gram Panchayat
Panchayat Karmi	The person who works as the Secretary of the Gram Panchayat
Panchayat Raj	Traditional institution of local rural self-governance
Samajik Nyay Samiti	Social Justice Committee
Samiti	A committee
Sanshodhan	Amendment
Sarpanch	The head of a Gram Panchayat
Sarvjanik Sampada Samiti	Common Resources Committee
Sharam Kosh	Labour Account
Shiksha Samiti	Education Committee
Swasthya Samiti	Health Committee
Tehsildar	Officer-in-charge of a tehsil

Tehsil	An administrative category denoting a revenue zone much smaller than a district
Up-sarpanch	Deputy head of the Gram Panchayat, elected among the Panchas of a Panchayat
Vastu Kosh	Material Account
Zilla Panchayat	The highest tier of the Panchayat Raj, formed at the district level

Acronyms and Abbreviations

BPL	Below Poverty Line
BDO	Block Development Office
CDP	Community Development Programme
CEO	Chief Executive Officer
DRDA	District Rural Development Agency
GS	Gram Sabha
GP	Gram Panchayat
JP	Janpad Panchayat
MLA	Member of Legislative Assembly
MP	Member of Parliament
NES	National Extension Service
NGO	Non-Governmental Organisation
OBC	Other Backward Caste
PESA	Panchayat Extension to Scheduled Areas Act
PRIs	Panchayat Raj Institutions
SC	Scheduled Caste, as per Articles 341 and 342 of the Constitution of India
ST	Scheduled Tribe, as per Articles 341 and 342 of the Constitution of India
SFC	State Finance Commission
ZP	Zilla Panchayat

1

Introduction

India, an ancient civilisation, witnessed the panchayats as an integral part of Indian society and polity since ages. Indian villages have been organised and maintained social order through panchayats since ancient times. The informal institution of panchayat was responsible for maintaining and governing village society in accordance with the socio-political norms of their times (Kashyap, 2003). Indian villages, remote and disconnected from the centres of power decided with a sense of autonomy their agenda of development and management of society and its resources with the institution of panchayat.

Panchayat Raj, as a system of governance at the grassroots level in rural India, has rightly been conceived as the most viable and proper mechanism of realising the goals of democracy and decentralisation (Joshi and Narwani, 2002). After independence efforts have been made to create the units of self-governance at grassroots level but all in vain since they could not produce the desired results. Also efforts were on to create the panchayats as units of self-governance but the committed Central Government's initiative came out with 73rd Amendment for the establishment of Panchayat Raj Institutions (PRIs) in India.

The 73rd Amendment to the Constitution of India not only gave a constitutional status to the panchayats; it also provided uniformity and formal structure to these traditional institutions of self-governance for the sake of their effective functioning. The earlier attempts at institutionalising the panchayats were half-hearted and failed due to the absence of supportive constitutional measures and lack of political will. The 73rd Amendment initiated a fundamental restructuring of governance and administrative system of the country, based on the philosophy of decentralisation and power to the people. The new Panchayat Raj institutions have the potential to usher in a new era of change and development in accordance with people's needs and priorities, and to revitalise a deeply troubled system of democracy (Behar and Kumar, 2002).

The pioneering and innovative initiatives of Madhya Pradesh government in strengthening and institutionalising decentralised rural self-governance in the post 73rd Amendment phase generated immense interest among the observers and experts who were keen to understand this significant change in the pattern of governance at the grassroots level.

In the continuation of the process of strengthening decentralised governance at local level, an innovation of Gram Swaraj system was introduced on 26 January, 2001. In this context, it became imperative to go beyond the government's stated objectives, rules and regulations, Acts and claims of effective functioning of panchayats, and takes an objective look at the ground reality and also to understand and analyse the innovations made by the State Government through Gram Swaraj.

Madhya Pradesh was the pioneer state, which implemented the 73rd Amendment by enacting panchayat law, and conducted panchayat elections in 1994. The Panchayat Raj system in Madhya Pradesh has constantly evolved during the past ten plus years, supported by a strong political will. There were several amendments to the Act and government orders issued over the past ten years, which supported and strengthened the decentralisation process. The Panchayat Raj system in Madhya Pradesh has a dynamic growth, which has constantly responded to the needs emerging from the field. Through Panchayat Raj, an attempt is being made to initiate a new era of people's empowerment. This amendment to the Panchayat Act to introduce the Gram Swaraj system clearly demonstrated this flexibility and commitment. Importantly, the Madhya Pradesh government perceived decentralisation and people's participation as central to its governance agenda, of which the panchayat system is a living example of democracy at the grassroots level.

Background

Historically, the institution of panchayat has been an integral part of rural Indian polity and society. Traditionally, panchayats have operated at two levels in the villages. The first level was that of the caste panchayats and the second was Gram Panchayat. Caste has been the predominant social reality of India, which dictated the organising principles of polity and society. Panchayat is no exception to this social reality. Different castes in the villages have different panchayats of their own. This tradition of caste panchayats is still prevalent on a large scale in India. However, issues having wider ramifications beyond the caste group were also discussed threadbare in the Gram Panchayats. These traditional panchayats played the vital role of maintaining socio-ethical norms and order, and dispensing justice. It also resolved, with all its inherent limitations, unforeseen crises and disputes, and took decisions on behalf of the village community for the welfare and development of the villages. Nevertheless, the process of decision-making was participatory and very often a democratic consensus emerged due to the mediation of the panchayat. This apparent democratic consensus was obviously limited and restricted within the framework of a hierarchical society divided on feudal and caste lines. Significantly, the panchayats derived their legitimacy from the support of the village community and its decisions were accepted as binding on the community.

Forces of modernism, coupled with the penetrative reach of the modern administrative paraphernalia under the colonial state, started drastically altering the cultural, socio-political and economic profile of Indian villages. This deeply affected the village institutions including panchayats. The modern state with the support of the bureaucratic framework slowly delegitimised informal institutions deriving legitimacy through informal channels. The growing functions of the state and its ever-increasing sphere also reduced the space of the panchayats. At this time, the Indian nationalist critique of colonialism emerged largely from a modernist paradigm and it largely used non-traditional instruments and strategies for the national movement. The cumulative result of the emergence of such forces of modernism was that the panchayats were reduced to playing a marginal role in the village society.

The Indian National Movement was deeply influenced by Gandhi's leadership and philosophy of non-violent civil disobedience, but the task of nation building was not undertaken in accordance with his philosophy. Gandhi's doctrine of nation building and national development was based on the concept of a confederation of villages; the model derived its roots from the traditional panchayat system. He envisaged greater autonomy to villages under a five-tier system of village panchayats, taluka panchayats, district panchayats, provincial panchayats and all-India panchayats. His concept of administrative/state system was based on a pyramid model whose broad base was composed of numerous village communities of India. The higher panchayats would help the village panchayats in areas where the village panchayat needed help and guidance for improving the system of public service. The fundamental unit of administration was village panchayat; the model suggested a bottom-up approach where the power flows upward from the smaller unit to the higher one.

The experience of partition and the centrifugal political forces during the struggling days of Indian independence forced India to adopt a strong two-tier federal structure with a tilt towards centralism. Pursuing a modernist paradigm, independent India's first Prime Minister, Pandit Jawaharlal Nehru, started creating and establishing new modern institutions and structures. His approach to nation building and national reconstruction was primarily top-down and for this he assigned a central role to the state. According to Nehru, the state could take on the task of nation building and also be the agent of social change. His faith in socialism and the process of planning led ultimately to a system, which was based on centralisation of power and authority. As a result the Gandhian paradigm of development, discussed above, was marginalised. Another important reason for this marginalisation was Dr. Ambedkar's views on Indian villages. He was primarily responsible for drafting the Constitution; he condemned the villages as "a sink of localism and a den of ignorance and narrow mindedness and communalism" (Ambedkar, 1948). Dr. Ambedkar felt that the Gandhian notion of village republic would adversely affect the country, therefore the idea of panchayats as fundamental unit of governance was rejected.

A middle path between these conflicting ideologies was devised and a mere formal acceptance of the idea of local autonomy and local self-governance was reflected in the incorporation of village panchayats in the directive principles of the Indian Constitution.

Initiatives for Panchayat Raj since Independence

Independent India inherited in 1947 a local self-government as a small wing of the local level of the governmental system. The major wing was the district administration, which was a complex of field offices and agencies of the then existing provincial government. District administration evolved structure, power and functions over long years in the initial three decades. It is now studded with manifold responsibilities relating to general administration, regulatory administration, revenue administration and development administration.

During this period, most of the provincial governments passed fresh laws for providing democratisation of structure and substantial enhancement of the powers of the local bodies. Administrative action also began to expand substantially the number of local bodies so as to cover increasing parts of the country. Several princely states then in existence in India also began to set up gradually local bodies, though with partial democratic structure and limited powers (Khanna, 1994).

Rural Local Self-Government during First Decade in Independent India

The first decade of Indian independence was mainly devoted to reorganisation of states and to develop certain legislative and administrative measures with a view to expand and develop rural local self-government. In this connection three main influences tended to make an impact upon policy makers. One was the viewpoint of Mahatma Gandhi who had been pleading over the years that village panchayats should be treated as the primary units of grassroots democracy. Another was that of newly framed democratic constitution of the country in which was a concrete provision about state's duty to develop panchayats as local self-governing units. The third was that of the viewpoint of the recently launched Five-Year Plans (1951 onwards) that people's participation should be promoted in management of rural development through local representative institutions. These three influences have continued to motivate, of course with fluctuating intensity, the policy makers and public leaders even subsequently.

A very significant influence with regard to development of rural local self-government over the years on government and public leaders has been of Mahatma Gandhi, the father of the Indian nation. In his writings and statements he always drew attention of the people and government to the urgent need for rebuilding the villages as self-sufficient and self-reliant entities with the village panchayat playing the central role in encouraging and supporting constructive and creative activities among the people. His dictum was "greater the power of the panchayat, the better for the people". He believed that true democracy "has to be worked from below by the people of every village".

The Constitution of India, promulgated in January 1950 for setting up a democratic and semi-federal political system, included Article 40 relating to the panchayats. Though the draft

Constitution did not include any mention about panchayats, some prominent members of the Constituent Assembly, influenced with Gandhian philosophy regarding self-governing villages, succeeded in getting it included in the final draft. Article 40 in the chapter on Directive Principles of State Policy states that "the State should take steps to organise village panchayats and endow them with such powers and authority as may be necessary to enable them to function as units of self-government". This constitutional directive tended to inspire the Union and State Governments to think about adoption of measures for development of the panchayats in the country. During the first decade of independent India fresh laws were passed in many states to democratise the structure, devolve more powers and expand the spatial coverage of the panchayats. More recently, this constitutional directive has been interpreted as empowering the government to provide constitutional sanction for important features of not only village panchayats but also of local self-governing bodies above it.

The era of planned development in India started in the fifties with the launching of the First Five-Year Plan in 1951-52. Since then development plans have been growing in dimensions, scope, diversity and complexities. Certain administrative changes within the governmental system have been brought about for their formulation and implementation at national, state and local levels. One of these changes relates to devolution of politico-administrative powers. These include strengthening of local self-government to play a meaningful role in local development processes. People's participation through representative local bodies is envisaged to energise these processes and also make them more relevant and responsive to people's needs and expectations.

Community Development Programme (1952)

As a part of the planned development initiated in the country, the first major rural development programme, named as Community Development Programme (CDP), was launched by the State Governments at some places in 1952 and later extended to many parts of the country in a phased manner. The basic premise on which CDP rests is to motivate the rural people to undertake self-reliant community-based approach for the improvement of economic and social condition of their life and environment. The government is expected to provide general guidance and technical-cum-financial assistance for reinforcing the community welfare programmes and activities, as need be. A few years later a programme with limited scope and funding named as National Extension Service (NES) was introduced as a prelude to the launching of CDP in the remaining parts of the country.

A new basic administrative unit below the district level, named as development block, was created in an increasing number to cover most parts of the country. Headed administratively by a block development officer and comprising several subject specialist extension officers, this new administrative unit was to serve as the locale of the CDP and NES under the overall direction of the district administration. For providing people's participation in local planning and implementation of these two programmes – one advisory committee of nominated persons was set up at the development block and another at district level. Certain administrative changes were also brought about at the level of the State Government, which had the main responsibility for these programmes under the overall guidance, support and review, by the Union Government.

Genesis of Panchayat Raj (1957-61)

During the closing years of the decade of 1950s it began to cause increasing concern to Union Government that due care was not being taken in avoiding wastage of funds in implementation of Community Development and allied programmes. This wastage was attributed to inefficiency in the implementation process. The National Development Council appointed a Committee on Plan Projects to look into this problem. The Committee appointed a Study Team in 1956 under the chairmanship of a senior legislator, Balwant Rai Mehta, to review critically the Community Development Projects and National Extension Service and suggest measures needed for effecting economy and improving efficiency in their implementation. The Team was also asked to examine: "the extent to which Community Development Movement has succeeded in utilising local initiatives and in creating institutions to ensure continuity in the process of improving economic and social conditions in rural areas".

The Planning Commission had already been advocating that village panchayats should be strengthened and linked with popular organisation at higher levels and that this new democratic set-up should gradually be given responsibility for taking over development administration and even some aspects of general administration within a district. The Mehta Committee kept this plea in view while formulating its own recommendations about reorganisation of institutional arrangements for community development and allied programmes.

In 1958, the Standing Committee of the National Development Council agreed broadly with the recommendations of the Study Team. It also recognised that since conditions varied in different parts of the country, the State Government concerned should be free to decide about the exact application of the concept of democratic decentralisation and its institutional set-up. The Union Government tried through holding meetings of State ministers and administrators as well as through convening conferences of All India Local Self-Government Council and Community Development Administrators to persuade, guide and support the State Government to establish the proposed system with any minor modifications as need be. The main purpose was to switch over to an institutionalised participative approach for rural development at local levels. Starting with the setting up of the new system by three State Governments in 1959, it was established in most of the existing states, with some variations in its structure, during the early part of the 1960s.

V.P. Naik Committee Report (1961)

In the state of Maharashtra a committee was set up by the State Government under V.P. Naik to recommend institutional set-up suited to the State for practical application of the concept of democratic decentralisation. The Report pointed out that people had yet to realise the importance of their role in "building up of the nation and its material prosperity". In order to enable them to play this role appropriately, local bodies at village, block and district levels should be set up. These bodies should be responsible to the people, enjoy their full confidence and be capable of enlisting their real, whole-hearted and determined support. Development functions needed to be separated into a local sector and a state sector. Popular local bodies at the village, block and district levels should play 'a vital role' in the local sector of development functions. It was the Committee's view that powers and resources should be largely devolved upon the local body at the district level, i.e., Zilla Parishad, as at that level mature representative leadership and adequately trained administrative personnel would be available. The Zilla Parishad, according to the Committee, should be broad based in composition through providing for a majority of its members to be directly elected. All district level development departments would have to be transferred to its control to provide administrative assistance. The panchayats would continue to function at village levels, revamped as need be, under the overall guidance of the Zilla Parishad. The Panchayat Samiti would act mainly as a statutory committee of the Zilla Parishad for implementing programmes assigned to it by the Parishad.

Since the end of 1959 a network of Panchayat Raj Institutions (PRIs) was built by most of the State Governments guided and supported by the Union Government and inspired as well by the Planning Commission. The three-tier Panchayat Raj system with powers largely devolved upon the Panchayat Samiti (the intermediate level body) with some adjustments became popular, by and large, with State Governments. After 1961, however, the recommendations of the Naik Committee of Maharashtra tended also to influence to a varied extent the decisions of some State Governments regarding distribution of devolved powers among the three levels within the Panchayat Raj system. However, most of the State Governments did not accept the Mehta Team's recommendations about District Collector being the chairman of Zilla Parishad. By

1964-65 Panchayat Raj began to function in most of the rural areas of 12 out of 15 states of India. Hardly any headway was made in the then existing Union Territories, except in one.

The lead in establishment of the Panchayat Raj was taken by the States of Rajasthan, Andhra Pradesh and Tamil Nadu in 1959. Prime Minister, Jawaharlal Nehru, went himself to Rajasthan to inaugurate it. This lead in Panchayat Raj was followed by a number of other states during the next few years, as the result of growing enthusiasm among the State Governments for the Panchayat Raj, which was expected to contribute significantly to the economic and social transformation of the depressed classes of rural life and environment. In Assam, Karnataka, Orissa, Punjab and Uttar Pradesh, it was established in 1960-61 by the governments concerned with some adaptations to suit their local needs. Next came Maharashtra, Gujarat, Bihar, Madhya Pradesh and West Bengal for launching it. The states of Kerala and Jammu and Kashmir, however, decided not to have the multi-tiered Panchayat Raj and only devolved some more powers to the existing village panchayats to perform a few developmental functions, besides the usual civic functions.

Stagnation and Decline (1965-85)

During the next two decades, however, Panchayat Raj began to stagnate in the first few years (1965-70) and then started even declining in efficacy of its role in promotion and management of development processes in the rural areas. This trend continued till 1985. Its public image and credibility began to suffer a set back. Its powers and functions were reduced by executive orders of the government on grounds of inefficiency.

The growing indifference of the State Governments and also of the Union Government in regard to development of Panchayat Raj was also attributable to certain happenings. One of these was that with the demise of Prime Minister Nehru in 1964 and also of several other panchayat prone political leaders and ministers, Panchayat Raj began to lose its ardent supporters. Several new ministers and many legislators began to develop increasing allergies with regard to the Panchayat Raj, as they tended to apprehend a challenge to their position from the emergent Panchayat Raj leadership, particularly at the Zilla Parishad and Panchayat Samiti levels.

Another reason was that the growing concern for improving the food grains production in the food-deficit country led to introduction of some new agriculture programmes. These were the Intensive Agriculture District Programme (1961), Intensive Agriculture Areas Programme (1963) and the High Yielding Variety (HYV) Programme (1965). These programmes were not entrusted to PRIs but were administrated directly by the Agriculture Department with the support of the District Collector. Even the existing agricultural personnel deputed to work under Panchayat Raj for promoting agricultural production as a part of Community Development Programme were withdrawn by the State Government's Department of Agriculture. Thinking that development targets could be achieved faster through bureaucratic administration under ministerial direction in the agricultural sector, a trend emerged within the State Governments to start withdrawing several other developmental functions along with their assigned personnel from the Panchayat Raj. This resulted in the weakening of the status and authority of the Panchayat Raj and steep falling off in its budget and staffing strength. Thus, panchayat began to drift into background in the context of growing sectoral development programmes promoted by governmental agencies.

During the decade of the seventies (even in 1969) the political situation underwent a change. There was an atmosphere of 'political uncertainty'. There was some weakening of political stability of State Governments in the country. Several State Governments and individual ministers concerned about stability of their office began to perceive increasingly serious challenges to their position from the ambitions of Panchayat Samiti, more so of Zilla Parishad members and chairmen. To ensure support of the legislators for their position, they tried to please them by repressing the role of the Panchayat Raj leadership of which these legislators began to be jealous politically.

Another cause of this decline of Panchayat Raj, was growing resentment of the common people against elite domination of it who tried to grabbing, by and large, benefits accruing from its working. As political awareness began to grow among these people on account of political processes at work with increasing intensity over the years, they began to resent elite domination and pleaded to keep them aloof from these institutions. Thus, Panchayat Raj was getting alienated from the majority of people in many states. Even in Maharashtra and Gujarat wherein Panchayat Raj had built a good image and credibility, it started stagnating to some extent. Luckily, however, in one state the moribund Panchayat Raj began to be gradually rejuvenated from 1978 onwards. The Left Front government in West Bengal started this process of rejuvenation partly to help the common people and partly to consolidate its own position politically.

In 1977 the Janata Party replaced the ruling Congress Party in the states as well as at the Union level. The Janata Party government appointed a high level committee under the chairmanship of an eminent legislator, Ashoka Mehta to inquire into the cause of decline in the working of Panchayat Raj with a view to recommending appropriate measures to reform and rejuvenate it.

Ashoka Mehta Committee Recommendations (1977-78)

The committee headed by a distinguished public leader like Ashoka Mehta was appointed by Janata Party government at the Centre in 1977 to inquire into the working of the PRIs and suggest measures to strengthen them, "so as to enable a decentralised system of planning and development to be effective". The Committee submitted its report next year. It mentioned that Panchayat Raj had been weakened due to certain adverse factors. Its structure was inadequate and government support meagre to enable it to perform developmental role effectively in a changing socio-economic environment since its inception in the early part of the decade of 1960s. In Maharashtra and Gujarat, however, PRIs were performing their role well on account of structural adequacy and appropriate State Government support. Elsewhere, degrading factors like political factionalism, oligarchic domination, corruption, inefficiency, parochial loyalties, power intoxication and political and bureaucratic apathy and arbitrariness had diluted its performance efficacy and public credibility.

The Committee made a number of recommendations to reform and revitalise Panchayat Raj based upon the central premise of "linking institutions of democratic decentralisation with socially motivated economic development". The Panchayat Raj structures, powers and functions and also relation with the government as well as with various relevant local institutions should be reviewed periodically and revised to enable it to perform its role effectively in the changing social and economic environments.

Though the recommendations of the Committee were not accepted by the Union Government due to change again in the ruling party within it, some of these did exercise varying influence upon the working of Panchayat Raj in a few states. Some years later (1983-85), Karnataka and Andhra Pradesh remodelled by and large their respective Panchayat Raj systems under this influence.

Renovation and Revival since 1985

Since the middle of the decade of 1980s there has been growing interest within the Union Government and within several State Governments in reviving the role of the Panchayat Raj, which had been languishing for a long time in many states in the country. The Planning Commission also reiterated its plea in the Five-Year Plans (Seventh and Eighth) for expanding and energising the role of Panchayat Raj in the promotion and management of rural development, which was now growing considerably in scope, diversity and complexity. Effective people's participation through Panchayat Raj in rural development according to the Commission, would contribute to better responsiveness to people's needs and aspirations and also to the coordinated and accelerated progress of this development.

One important step taken by the Union Government in 1984, the Prime Minister wrote to Chief Ministers of State Governments to take appropriate action without further delay for holding of overdue elections to PRIs as well as for revitalising their functioning. Another important step taken by this government was to appoint two committees successively in 1985 and 1986 respectively to suggest ways and means for strengthening Panchayat Raj as vibrant local institutional set-up for playing an active and purposeful role in management of local services and appropriate development programmes. One committee under the chairmanship of a senior administrator (G.V.R. Rao) reported in 1985, suggesting appropriate improvement in the representative character and strengthening of the capability of both the people's representatives and the administrative personnel in the PRIs so as to equip them to play a more active, equitable and efficient role in promoting and managing rural development and local affairs.

The other committee under the chairmanship of a distinguished jurist (L.M. Singhvi) advocated that Panchayat Raj should primarily be viewed as the local self-government system. It should be strengthened so as to serve better as one of the foundation stones of the country's democratic political system. Its secondary role of much importance was to continue to be that of an administrative agency for promotion and management of rural development. In order to strengthen the status of Panchayat Raj its main features should be mentioned in the Constitution itself. The existing constitutional provision (Article 40) is too general and also of discretionary nature to provide appropriately a firm basis to Panchayat Raj system which had been weakened largely on account of neglect and unscrupulous politicking in various states.

The Union Government also convened workshops of senior administrators concerned with Panchayat Raj affairs to provide opportunity to them to express their views about reinforcing and reorienting Panchayat Raj for undertaking increasing responsibility for management of local development and local affairs.

The administrators agreed that Panchayat Raj based upon the concept of democratic decentralisation within the country's governmental system needed to be revamped suitably to improve its working for accelerating responsive and equitable development processes as well as for contributing to development of citizenship standards.

Conferences of Panchayat Raj leaders (including women) were as well arranged by the government to elicit their views about reorganisation and strengthening of Panchayat Raj. In these conferences the demand was for debureaucratisation of the control of Panchayat Raj as well as for devolution of more powers and resources to it.

Taking into account the views of these committees, workshops and conferences, the Union Government decided to amend the Constitution of the country in order to provide a firm constitutional basis to the essential features of the Panchayat Raj. This was intended to provide substantial protection to Panchayat Raj against negligence or arbitrary action by State Governments, which had been contributing to its emasculation in many states over the years. It is as recently as 1992 that the government finally succeeded in getting the amendment approved by the Parliament. The State Governments were required to take appropriate action under it.

Re-establishment of Panchayat Raj Institutions (1992)

As described earlier, in the 1990s, there had been growing serious concern in the country with regard to the weak status of the Panchayat Raj in most of the states. It was widely recognised by the government, public leaders, intelligentsia that the PRIs were not able to "acquire the status and dignity of viable and responsive people's bodies". The main reasons mentioned by the government and others for this were: "absence of regular elections, prolonged super sessions, insufficient representation of weaker sections like Scheduled Castes/Scheduled Tribes and women, inadequate devolution of powers and lack of financial resources".

Though Article 40 of the Constitution has directed the Indian State to organise and empower village panchayats to enable them to function as "units of self-government", most of the State Governments have actually tended to pay only half-hearted attention to this directive. The Union Government therefore has stated the imperative need to "enshrine in the constitution certain basic and essential features of the Panchayat Raj institutions to impart certainty, continuity and strength to them".

The 64th Constitutional Amendment Bill suggested setting up of panchayats in every state at the village level, intermediate level and district level. The intermediate level was not obligatory in the states with a population of less than 20 lakhs. This bill was passed in the Lok Sabha in 1989 but could not be passed by the Rajya Sabha. The 73rd Constitutional Amendment Bill (1990) was introduced in the Lok Sabha and recommended that Gram Sabha should be constituted in each village in addition to the panchayats at three levels. The bill recommended that the elections to the village panchayat should be direct and at other levels at least 50 per cent of seats should be directly elected. This bill also lapsed.

For this purpose the 73rd Constitution Amendment Act, 1992 was passed by the Union Parliament. In the Constitution, Part IX and Schedule XI have been inserted to contain certain provisions for the panchayats from the village to the sub-district and district levels.

Context of the 73rd Amendment

It has been made clear that various committees and sub-committees had made several recommendations and proposals for institutionalising the Panchayat Raj system and these efforts culminated in the form of the 73rd Constitutional Amendment providing constitutional status to the PRIs. The explanation for the easy passage of the 73rd Amendment Bill and the acceptance of radical restructuring of the state structure with far-reaching political consequences goes way beyond the committee reports and proposals. To comprehend the dynamics of change it is imperative to understand the context of this amendment.

Several decades of centralised planning and a top-down model of development had paid dividends in terms of economic growth and industrialisation. This development model was adopted with the hope that the trickle-down effect will involve the poor and the marginalised in the process of development. Unfortunately, this trickle down did not take place and a distorted and lopsided development process emerged, where the resources and authority became further concentrated in a few hands. The fruits of development were neither shared, nor did the poor and marginalised had access to it. The marginalised sections (the poor, women or rural people) continued to be marginalised. It was clear by the 1980s that for more egalitarian and balanced development to be achieved, a more participative, democratic and decentralised bottom-up model of development was needed.

Many of these discourses propounded that for achieving the objectives of democratic states, the governance systems needed substantial changes, making the structure more participative and decentralised. The paradigmatic shift was evident in the attempts to transform governance to enhance accountability and projects to reinvent government and the bureaucracy. The dictum that "lesser governance is better governance" was used to restructure governments and enhance their efficacy through moves towards decentralisation, ending 'licence raj' and reducing the government's regulatory functions.

During the late 1970s and 1980s all over the world and especially in India, various social movements and civil society initiatives were trying to reclaim their legitimate space from the state. These new social movements and civil society actors were generating and spreading democratic consciousness among the people with a view to suggesting that a democratic development process had to be participative and bottom-up. According to them, development had to be based on local needs, priorities and micro-initiatives. Development should be a flexible process emanating from the grassroots level and not a blue print given from above. For these ends, the social movements and civil society actors were demanding radical changes in the governmental structure, to make it more participative, decentralised, democratic, accountable and transparent. The underlying theme was to replace the state-centric development process with a people-centric development process.

Under the impact of such changing context the Indian State was under increasing pressure to radically restructure its governance system to make it more democratic and participative and to address the needs and priorities of the marginalised sections of the society. It was genuinely felt that a more grassroots approach would enhance the efficacy of the state's planning and implementation machinery and incorporate the marginalised and underprivileged in the mainstream of development. At this juncture the political will and support at the highest level also played a crucial role in preparing the ground for a Panchayat Raj system. Once brought to the forefront, the political parties understood the implications and potential of the Panchayat Raj system and a political consensus emerged in favour of empowering the Panchayat Raj system.

The 73rd Amendment

The 73rd Amendment Bill was passed by the Lok Sabha and the Rajya Sabha with near unanimity on the 22 and 23 December, 1992 respectively. This bill was ratified by 17 State Assemblies in 1993 and came into force as Constitution (73rd Amendment) Act from 24 April, 1993. The Act provides constitutional status to the panchayats and gives it uniformity by making the three-tier system a permanent feature. The key features of the Act are as follows:

- Panchayats shall be constituted in every state at the village, intermediate and district level. However, the states with a population not exceeding 20 lakhs have been given the option not to have any intermediate level panchayat.
- There shall be a Gram Sabha in each village exercising such powers and performing such functions at the village level as the legislature of a state may provide by law.
- Members of panchayats at all levels will be elected through direct elections. The election of the chairperson at the intermediate and district level will be through indirect elections

and the mode of election of the chairperson of the village panchayat has been left to the respective states.

- Seats are reserved for Scheduled Castes (SCs) and Scheduled Tribes (STs) at all levels according to their population at each level. Not less than one-third of seats are reserved for women and these may be allotted by rotation. The office of chairperson will also be subject to this provision.
- A uniform five-year term has been granted to the Panchayats. In case of dissolution or being superseded, elections should be held within six months of the date of dissolution.
- State legislatures have the legislative power to confer on the panchayats such powers and authority as may be necessary to enable them to function as institutions of self-governance. They may be entrusted with the responsibility of (i) preparing plans for social justice and economic development; (ii) implementation of schemes for social justice and economic development; and (iii) in regard to matters listed in the 11th schedule. The list contains 29 items, such as land improvement, minor irrigation, fisheries, education, women and child development.
- State Government has the power to authorise the panchayats to levy, collect and appropriate suitable local taxes. The government can make grant-in-aid to the panchayats from the consolidated fund of the concerned state.
- Review of the financial position of the panchayats will be undertaken by a finance commission, which shall be constituted every five years. It will also make recommendations on the distribution of funds between state and local bodies.
- A State Election Commission shall be constituted to ensure free and fair elections to the panchayats.

The 73rd Amendment was inserted in Part IX of the Constitution, containing Article 243 to 243-O. Local government is an exclusive state subject under entry 5 of List II of the 7th Schedule, therefore the Union just provides the outline of the panchayat system, which would be implemented by the states by making laws or amending their existing laws to bring them in conformity with the provisions of the 73rd Amendment. It was binding on the states that the implementing legislation should be undertaken within a year of the commencement of the 73rd Amendment Act.

Panchayat Raj in Madhya Pradesh

In the post-73rd Amendment phase different States have responded with varying degrees of enthusiasm. Madhya Pradesh responded with innovativeness and remarkable commitment to making the system sustainable and successful. The state's effort to institutionalise the system is evident in the number of amendments that have been made to the State Panchayat Act as a dynamic response to the problems at the ground level. During the implementation of the Panchayat Raj system, Madhya Pradesh has faced several opportunities and difficulties. The experience of the state is extremely rich and provides vital insights into the process of institutionalising Panchayat Raj. On the negative side, is the story of bureaucratic resistance, functional problems, political and institutional challenges, financial inadequacy and mismatch of capacities and roles. On the other hand, it involves the grassroots people in a democratic and participative governance system, and therefore potentially unleashes its considerable energy.

The Gram Sabha at the lowest rung of village is the first modern political institution, which seeks to place direct political power in the hands of people, without the mediation of elected representatives. The vision of Gram Sabha in a village situation can be compared with the Parliament and Assembly. Gram Sabha is the most powerful foundation of decentralised governance but unfortunately it could not become a vibrant and important institution at grassroots level because of local leadership and bureaucracy. Mostly Gram Sabhas were dominated by 'Sarpanchas' and a small group of their associates.

Participation in Gram Sabha meetings has been low. Low participation can be mainly attributed to the strong and invincible caste, class and gender divide in villages. Sarpanch and other influential people dominate in decision-making process. Two prominent and sharply contrasting groups leading the panchayats-one is group of traditionally influential representatives and other that of new entrants. The performance and efficacy of panchayat members is strongly influenced by the caste and class distinctions. Gram Panchayats are not adequately accountable to Gram Sabha. The Gram Sabha is not aware of the Gram Panchayat functioning. The concept of participation as an important part of Panchayat Raj has been rarely seen in practice. In fact, in retrospect, it seems inevitable that persons of influence would look at larger community participation with hostility.

Gram Sabha or people's forum has always been an integral part of the concept of a Gram Panchayat. Rajni Kothari visualises Gram Sabha as 'watchdogs' coming between the politician-bureaucratic nexus. "The only way of making this nexus responsible and accountable is to provide larger citizen involvement in new variants of old institutions like the Gram Sabha which can combine older forms of informal consensus-making mechanisms with the more formal, institutionalised and legal forms decreed by legislation. With the new awakening in the rural areas, these bodies have the potential of overseeing the working of elected bodies and over time with growing confidence that they cannot be browbeaten by dominant individuals or castes, become a force to reckon with" (Kothari, 1998). It is unfortunate that both grassroots leadership and grassroots bureaucracy could not strengthen the Gram Sabha. The institution of Gram Sabha has become dysfunctional due to lack of leverage of local leaders to initiate meaningful participation in the sabha and their incapability to persuade people to support local initiatives (Fernandes, 1999). It has been evident that meetings called were mostly without prior and adequate notice. In most places, only a formality was observed; at times proxy meetings were convened and proceedings were written even without the knowledge of those who attended. Meeting, if arranged, either proved to be abortive or unsuccessful because of thin attendance with the panchayat or discussion (Mander, 1999).

The vibrancy and efficacy of Gram Sabha will remain dismal if it does not posses the capacity to perform assigned roles and responsibility. This question becomes more pertinent in a socio-cultural milieu where human resource development is low and society is deeply fragmented and hierarchical.

The State Government was unhappy with Gram Panchayats mainly because they tend be dominated by Sarpanchs and small groups of their associates. The then Chief Minister Digvijay Singh was said to have remarked, "I did not expect Panchayat Raj to become Sarpanch Raj" (Manor, 2001). Decentralised governance at grassroots level has given both positive and negative signs and in Madhya Pradesh, Gram Swaraj has emerged after an extensive process of deliberations, refinements and dialogue. It is also a result of the grassroots experiences of functioning of Panchayat Raj coupled with Madhya Pradesh government's stated commitment to democratic decentralisation. The Gandhian ideological framework provided the basic structure and body to this new system of self-governance (Behar, 2001).

It is certain that unless we have a vibrant Gram Sabha, we cannot have empowered and accountable panchayats (Nambiar, 2001). In tribal regions the Gram Sabhas are empowered with all powers since 1997 but a study concludes that the people at large are least informed (Sisodia, 2002). At the micro level, the Gram Sabha is a people's institution and has been made a statutory body through a Constitutional Amendment. Gram Swaraj system has provided all powers and duties to Gram Sabha. The resource flow to Gram Sabha and its ever-increasing powers and authority have generated a lot of interest in people. This interest is likely to translate into a more broad based and participative leadership at grassroots level.

The above analysis clearly indicates that the Gram Sabhas are entrusted with all powers and duties but the experience of previous years depicts a very disappointing picture. Panchayats at grassroots levels in Madhya Pradesh had witnessed low participation of stake-holders and the implementation of Gram Swaraj is the obvious result of it.

Against this backdrop, it was very important to conduct a research study in the state of Madhya Pradesh, which could try to understand the ground realities of the new system. It will provide an insight along with problems and prospects of the new system. The output of the study will be of critical use for planners, policy makers and academicians.

It is extremely pertinent to study and document this process of transition in Madhya Pradesh. The process of implementation of the Gram Swaraj has raised several vital questions linked to the institutional and structural mechanism of governance. The PRIs also have far reaching implications for the political and social processes. Through a study on the functioning of Gram Swaraj in Madhya Pradesh, an attempt is made to comprehend and analyse these implications and processes.

This study is an attempt to identify, document and comprehend the broad trends emanating from the field, based on the experience of three years' functioning of Gram Swaraj in Madhya Pradesh. Three years is a short span of time for the dust to settle from such radical changes. However, it is important to understand and analyse the process and direction of institutionalisation of the present system and its status in the initial phase (2001 to 2004), which would have a significant impact and critical lessons for charting out the future course of action for effective people-centric development and governance not only in the state but across the country.

This study is divided into seven chapters. First chapter provides detailed introduction of the study including the background of the Panchayat Raj in India. The second chapter elaborates the constitutional framework of Panchayat Raj in Madhya Pradesh including the amendment package of Gram Swaraj. Third chapter consists of study design. Fourth chapter documents the village situation and operationalisation of Gram Sabha. Chapter fifth interprets the perceptions and attitudes of panchayat representatives whereas chapter sixth analyses the perceptions and attitudes of Gram Sabha members. Chapter seventh concludes the study.

References

Ambedkar, B.R. (1948): Speech in the Constituent Assembly on November 14, 1948, in Vasant Moon (ed.) *Writings and Speeches*, 13: 61-61, Department of Education, Government of Maharashtra, Mumbai.

Behar, Amitabh (2001): "Madhya Pradesh Gram Swaraj: Experiment in Direct Democracy", *Economic and Political Weekly*, March 10.

Behar, Amitabh and Kumar, Yogesh (2002): "Decentralisation in Madhya Pradesh, India: from Panchayati Raj to Gram Swaraj (1995 to 2001)", *Working Paper 170*, ODI, London, UK.

Fernandes, A. (1999): "Reconnecting the Sabha to Gram", paper presented at the National Conference on Gram Sabha, National Institute of Rural Development, Hyderabad, July 28-29.

Joshi R.P. and Narwani G.S. (2002): *Panchayat Raj in India: Emerging Trends Across States*, Rawat Publications, Jaipur.

Kashyap, Subhash C. (2003): *Blueprint of Political Reform*, Shipra Publications, Delhi.

Khanna, B.S. (1994): *Panchayati Raj in India (Rural Local Self Government)*, Deep and Deep Publication, New Delhi.

Kothari, Rajni (1998): *State Against Democracy: In Search of Human Governance*, Ajanta Publications, Delhi.

Mander, Harsh (1999): "Towards Direct Democracy: The Legal Empowerment of Gram Sabha", *Kurukshetra*, New Delhi, Vol. 48, No. 1, October.

Manor, James (2001): "Madhya Pradesh Experiments with Direct Democracy", *Economic and Political Weekly*, March 3.

Nambiar, Malini (2001): "Making the Gram Sabha Work", *Economic and Political Weekly*, August 18.

Sisodia, Yatindra Singh (2002): "Decentralised Governance in Madhya Pradesh: Experiences of Gram Sabha in Scheduled Areas", *Economic and Political Weekly*, October 5.

2

Development of Panchayat Raj in Madhya Pradesh: From Beginning to Gram Swaraj

An Overview of Panchayat Raj in Madhya Pradesh

The traditional panchayats were vibrant in Madhya Pradesh. The tribes have had long traditional panchayats and their 'traditional' way of life was governed by these institutions. With modernisation and functioning of modern welfare state, the strength of the traditional panchayats has slowly diminished to some extent in the tribal areas of the State.

Efforts have been made by enacting laws that further the cause of decentralised governance. The Madhya Pradesh Panchayat Act, 1962 was one such effort based on the recommendations of the Balwant Rai Mehta Committee. A new Panchayat Raj Act was enacted in 1981, which was later amended in 1988 to provide reservations of seats for SCs, STs and women in panchayats. However, these institutions were given extremely restricted local-maintenance functions and had no developmental responsibilities, which made them largely ineffective. Elections to these bodies were not held regularly and the bodies remained under the control of government-appointed administrators.

The Madhya Pradesh Panchayat Raj Act, 1990 attempted to revitalise the Panchayat Raj Institutions (PRIs) and transfer power to the people to ensure their effective participation. The key features of this Act were direct elections to these bodies, involvement of political parties and the transfer of resources and developmental machinery to the panchayats.

The Madhya Pradesh Panchayat Raj Act, 1993 was enacted to cover the lacunae in existing laws for the establishment of panchayat institutions. This Act was drafted in conformity with the objectives, substance and directives of the 73rd Constitutional Amendment Act. The Act provides for a separate and independent audit organisation (under the control of the State Government) to monitor the audit of panchayat accounts; a State Election Commission to supervise, direct and control the preparation of electoral rolls and to conduct elections to the panchayats; and a State Finance Commission (SFC) to recommend to the State Government any grant-in-aid as may be needed by the panchayats. The Act was given Governor's assent on January 24th, 1994.

Panchayat Raj in Madhya Pradesh prior to 1990

Based on the recommendations of the Balwant Rai Mehta Committee, the Madhya Pradesh Panchayat Act, 1962, was enacted. It made provision for a three-tier structure of the PRIs in the state. These levels were: the Gram Panchayat at the village level; Janpad Panchayat at the block level; and the Zilla Panchayat at the district level. In Madhya Pradesh, the PRIs were not taken seriously and merely remained as legal bodies to be managed by the state bureaucracy. The state clearly lacked the administrative and political will to institutionalise and empower the local institutions of self-governance.

The Madhya Pradesh Panchayat Raj Act, 1990 attempted to revitalise PRIs and transfer 'power to people' as a prerequisite to democratic decentralisation. In the process, it devolved more powers to these institutions for promoting socio-economic development. This Act also attempted to ensure the effective participation of PRIs in local administration and developmental activities. A three-tier structure was proposed by the Act, comprising Gram Panchayats at the village level, Janpad Panchayats at the block level and Zilla Panchayats at the district level. The key new features of this Act were: direct elections to these bodies; involvement of political parties; transfer of resources and machinery to panchayats; and a Gram Sabha coterminous with a Patwari circle.

The Act apparently attempted to empower and strengthen the PRIs but failed in its stated objectives. The desire of the State Government not to devolve substantial powers, authority and resources to the PRIs (as in all previous attempts) in the absence of a constitutional decree was evident. Bureaucratic resistance, institutional unpreparedness and lack of political will explained this half-hearted attempt at institutionalising the PRIs. This background of resistance needs to be understood for any meaningful debate on the success of the post 73rd Amendment in the Panchayat Raj system of Madhya Pradesh.

Madhya Pradesh Panchayat Raj Act, 1993

The Madhya Pradesh Panchayat Raj Act, 1993 was enacted to create and amend existing laws for the establishment of PRIs. This Act was drafted in conformity with the objectives, substance and directives of the 73rd Constitutional Amendment. The Act was given Governor's assent on 24 January, 1994.

Objective of the Act

The primary objective of the Act is to strengthen and empower the PRIs and to ensure effective involvement of these institutions in local administration and development activities. The idea is to make PRIs more democratic through people's greater participation, democratic decentralisation and effective local self-governance, and with the help of agents of economic and social justice. This Act provides vital agencies and provisions for socio-economic changes and development in the sphere of panchayats in Madhya Pradesh in recent years. Here, an effort is made to provide an overview of the Panchayat Act, 1993.

Structure of the Gram Sabha

The Gram Sabha consists of all people in the voter list of every village or village cluster. A Gram Sabha should meet at least four times in a year; an extraordinary meeting can be called if required by the Janpad or Zilla Panchayat, Collector, or if one-third of the total members of the Gram Sabha request so in writing. The required quorum is one-tenth of the total members of the Gram Sabha. The Sarpanch or Up-sarpanch presides over the meeting and the Secretary of the Gram Panchayat convenes the meeting.

Structure of the Gram Panchayat

Each village or cluster of villages is required to have a Gram Panchayat with a tenure of five years. The Gram Panchayats are divided into a minimum of 10 wards, and if the population of the village is more than 1,000, the number of wards can be more than 10 but should not exceed 20. Every Gram Panchayat consists of elected panches from the wards, an elected Sarpanch and a Up-sarpanch. The seats to be filled by direct election in every Gram Panchayat are reserved for SCs and STs in proportion to their population in the Gram Panchayat, on a rotational basis. A Gram Panchayat with 50 per cent or less of seats reserved for both SCs and STs has 25 per cent seats reserved for the Other Backward Classes (OBCs) on a rotational basis. The Sarpanch is directly elected and is the key functionary of the system. Significantly, the Act reserves one-third of the total number of seats of Sarpanches within a block for women. This reservation for women is a reservation within a reservation for SC, ST and OBC seats, implying that one-third of these reserved seats will be reserved for women of these categories. The Up-sarpanch is elected from the elected Panches, and if the Sarpanch is not an SC or an ST, then the Up-sarpanch is elected from this category. A no-confidence motion against the Sarpanch and Up-sarpanch can be passed by a resolution with a majority of not less than three-quarters of Panches present and voting, and if such a majority is more than two-thirds of the total number of Panches constituting the Gram

Panchayat. A meeting of Gram Panchayat discussing a no-confidence motion is presided over by an officer of the government. Each Gram Panchayat is required to have standing committees not exceeding three, and these committees exercise powers as assigned by the Gram Panchayat. A Gram Panchayat creates a Gram Panchayat Fund, and all sums received by the panchayat are part of this fund. The fund is utilised for developmental activities of the panchayat, or for other expenses approved by the government. The State Government appoints a Secretary to a Gram Panchayat for keeping and maintaining records of the Gram Panchayat.

Structure of the Janpad Panchayat

The Janpad Panchayat, the second tier of the Panchayat Raj system, is constituted at the block level, and consists of members elected from the constituencies; members co-opted from the marketing societies or cooperatives, and all members of the State Legislative Assembly representing constituencies of the block. The government divides the constituencies for the Janpad Panchayat and each constituency has a population of not more than 5,000. The total number of constituencies should not exceed 25 and these are single-member constituencies. The reservation of seats for SCs, STs, OBCs and women is in accordance with the principle adopted for Gram Panchayat. Every Janpad Panchayat makes five standing committees from its members. These committees are General Administration Committee, Agriculture Committee, Education Committee, Communication and Works Committee and the Cooperation and Industries Committee. The Janpad Panchayat establishes a Janpad Panchayat fund similar to the Gram Panchayat Fund and the funds are utilised for developmental activity or other expenses as approved by the government. A Chief Executive Officer (CEO) appointed by the government will be responsible for keeping and maintaining the records of the Janpad Panchayat.

Structure of the Zilla Panchayat

Every district has a Zilla Panchayat with a term of five years, consisting of members elected from the constituencies; Chairperson of District Cooperatives and Development Bank; all members of the Lok Sabha representing the district partially or wholly; all members of State Legislative Assembly returned from districts; and members of Rajya Sabha returned from the state whose names appears in the voter list of a Gram Panchayat within the district. The government divides the constituencies; each constituency is a single member constituency and has a population of 50,000. The total number of constituencies does not exceed 35. The Chairperson and the Vice-Chairperson of the Zilla Panchayat are elected for five years and the procedure of election is similar to that of the Janpad Panchayat. Reservation of seats of Zilla Panchayat and for the office of Chairperson and the Vice-Chairperson of Zilla Panchayat is according to the principle adopted for reservation in Janpad Panchayat.

The Zilla Panchayat controls and supervises the administration of the District Rural Development Agency (DRDA) and all functions and schemes assigned to DRDA by the State Government should be implemented under the supervision of the Zilla Panchayats.

Zilla Panchayat Fund is created similar to the fund of Janpad Panchayat and the fund is utilised for developmental activity by the panchayats or other expenses approved by the government. A government appointee, called the Chief Executive Officer, acts as the Secretary of the Zilla Panchayat and is responsible for keeping and maintaining records.

Distribution of Functions, Powers and Tax Imposition

Gram Panchayat

Functions

Sanitation, construction and maintenance of sources of water, construction of roads, buildings, bridges, latrines, wells, lighting of village streets, control over entertainment shows, shops, eateries, maintenance of panchayat property, establishment and management of market and melas, prevention of contagious diseases, promotion of youth and property, promotion of youth and family welfare, etc.

Powers

Providing public health facility, control on erection of buildings and such building, fining obstruction and encroachment upon public streets or open spaces, to name buildings and streets, etc.

Tax

Property tax on land or buildings, tax on private latrines, lighting tax, professional tax, market fees, and fee on registration of cattle sold in any market under the control of Gram Panchayat.

Janpad Panchayat

Functions

Integrated Rural Development Programme (IRDP); agriculture; social forestry; cottage industries; family planning; sports; rural employment programme; provision for emergency relief in cases of fire, flood, drought, etc.; arrangement in connection with local pilgrimage and festivals; management of public ferries, public markets, melas, etc.; any other function with the approval of the State Government and the Zilla Panchayat.

Tax

Janpad Panchayat can impose tax on theatre and other public entertainment; fees for any licensee or permission granted by the Janpad Panchayat and for use and occupation of lands or other properties vested in or maintained by the Janpad Panchayat.

Zilla Panchayat

Functions

The functions and powers of the Zilla Panchayat are to control, coordinate and guide the Gram Panchayat and Janpad Panchayat within the district; coordinate and consolidate the Janpad Panchayat plans; coordinate the demands for grants for special purposes received from the Janpad Panchayats and forward them to the State Government; secure the execution of plans, projects, schemes or other works common to two or more Janpad Panchayats of the district; advise the State Government on social forestry, family welfare, welfare of the disabled, destitute, women, youth and children; exercise such other powers which the State Government entrusts to it.

Functioning of the Panchayats

The meetings of panchayats called by the Sarpanch or the President should be held every month, failing which the Secretary or the Chief Executive Officer (CEO) issues notice of the meeting 25 days after the last held panchayat meeting. The quorum of the panchayat meeting is half the members constituting the panchayat. If the quorum is not complete, then the competent authority postpones the meeting, and for such postponed meeting, a quorum is not required but no new subjects can be brought for consideration. A notice of the meeting is pasted at the panchayat office. The Secretary and the CEOs of the Janpad and Zilla Panchayat place a report about the income and expenditure of the Panchayat before the panchayat respectively.

The Madhya Pradesh Panchayat Raj Act, 1993, provides for a separate and independent audit organisation, i.e., the State Finance Commission, under the control of the State Government, to look after the audit of accounts of panchayats. The State Election Commission supervises, directs and controls the preparations of electoral rolls and conducts all elections to panchayats.

The State Government may vest in the panchayats any property vested with the State Government. It may assign to a panchayat such taxes, tolls, fees levied and collected by the State Government, and may make grant-in-aid from the consolidated fund of the state for such purposes and subject to such conditions and limits as the State Government may deem fit. The State

Government shall make grant-in-aid to the panchayats as may be decided on the recommendations of the State Finance Commission. The State Government is empowered to make rules to regulate the imposition, assessment, collection and sharing of taxes for panchayats. It can also dissolve panchayats for default or abuse of power. A dissolved panchayat is to be reconstituted within six months in accordance with the provisions of the Act. The State Government also regulates the relations between panchayats and other local authorities in matters in which they are jointly interested. The State Government makes the rules for implementing various provisions of this Act. It may, from time to time, make model by-laws for the guidance of panchayats.

Panchayat Raj system in Madhya Pradesh has not remained static but evolved in the last one decade. A dynamic and adaptive Panchayat Raj system has ensured the success of PRIs in the state. This adaptiveness is reflected in the various Amendments made to the Panchayat Raj Act, 1993, and the ever-evolving office orders issued to operationalise and institutionalise the Panchayat Raj system.

Amendments to the Madhya Pradesh Panchayat Raj Act, 1993

Several challenges to the Panchayat Raj system have emerged during the last one decade of its operationalisation in Madhya Pradesh. Fortunately, a proactive State Government has responded to these needs and challenges. The government analysed the strain on the system and identified the problem areas, and made a serious attempt to address these problem areas at all levels. The causative factors were identified in the underlying panchayat laws and the Panchayat Raj system as enunciated in the Madhya Pradesh Panchayat Raj Act, 1993. The State Government, in earnest to resolve these constraints, changed and reissued its office orders and also amended the Panchayat Act itself. This willingness and flexibility of the State Government to tackle bottlenecks has given strength to the Panchayat Raj system in Madhya Pradesh. It also reflects the political will to ensure the success of Panchayat Raj system in the state. The amendments have given much-needed elasticity to the system and have contributed to the success of the Panchayat Raj system in Madhya Pradesh as institutions of grass-roots democracy. A dynamic system where information flows upward from the bottom and a system that responds and adjusts to these stimuli is a truly democratic and representative system. The State Government has made more than ten amendments to the Madhya Pradesh Panchayat Act, 1993. Drawing on experience gathered in the functioning of the PRIs, the State Government has amended the Panchayat Act to genuinely strengthen and empower the Panchayat Raj system.

An analysis of the amendments clearly reflects the government's desire to institutionalise and empower the system. The amendments deal with the teething problems of the system. Via the amendments, the State Government has tried to overcome limitations that had cropped up during implementation of the Act. For example, it was realised that women did not attend the Gram Sabha despite it being a crucial forum for public debate and decision-making on village and panchayat issues. The lack of women's participation in Gram Sabha despite reservation for women in elected positions of panchayats was viewed detrimental to the objectives of Panchayat Raj. The Madhya Pradesh government therefore amended Article 6 of the State Panchayat Act to make it mandatory to have one-third of the quorum as women members. Another interesting example is the amendment of the Act, which barred any Member of Parliament (MP) or Member of the Legislative Assembly (MLA) who represents a completely urban constituency from being a member of the Zilla or Janpad Panchayat. This was clearly done to protect the interests of rural areas in relation to urban areas.

The aim, in addition to strengthening the panchayat, is also to articulate and define the functional space of these institutions. A constant endeavour was to define the function of these institutions and devolve more administrative and financial powers to the panchayats. Simultaneously, the amendments try to guarantee socio-economic change in favour of the marginalised, as envisaged in the 73rd Constitutional Amendment. The State Government, through the amendments, has tried to operationalise the panchayats, consistent with the ideology of 'power to people' and democratic decentralisation. The amendments made in the Panchayat Act in 2001 paved the way for the introduction of Gram Swaraj. This issue is discussed in details here.

The Madhya Pradesh Panchayat Raj (Sanasodhan) Adhiniyam, 2001

The amendment related to Gram Swaraj is discussed here in detail. Since the study is devoted to understand the Gram Swaraj, it would be appropriate to provide the detailed elaboration of the amendment package to interpret the prime motive behind extending direct democracy to the grassroots people.

Composition of Gram Sabha

There shall be a Gram Sabha for every village. The Gram Sabha shall be a body corporate by the name specified, therefore having perpetual succession and a common seal and shall by the said name sue and be sued and shall be subject to the provisions of this Act.

There shall be held at least one meeting in every month, of the Gram Sabha, which shall be convened by the Secretary of the Gram Sabha. The date, time and the place of the first meeting of the Gram Sabha shall be fixed by the Sarpanch.

Not less than one-fifth of the total number of members of the Gram Sabha shall form a quorum for a meeting of Gram Sabha, out of which not less than one-third shall be women members and members of Scheduled Castes (SCs) and Scheduled Tribes (STs) shall be represented in proportion to their population in the Gram Sabha. Quorum shall be necessary for every meeting of the Gram Sabha.

The meeting of the Gram Sabha shall be presided over by Sarpanch or in the absence of Sarpanch by Up-sarpanch. In the event of both Sarpanch and Up-sarpanch being absent, the meeting of the Gram Sabha shall be presided over by a Panch to be elected for such meeting.

Decision-making in Gram Sabha

If any dispute arises as to whether a person is entitled to attend a meeting of the Gram Sabha, the same shall be decided by the person presiding on the basis of the entry in the list of voters of the Gram Sabha area and his decision shall be final. Any dispute arising between Gram Sabhas or any matter concerning more than one Gram Sabha comprised within the area of Gram Panchayat and all matters contained shall be brought before a joint meeting of all Gram Sabhas.

The decision taken at the joint meeting shall be deemed to be the decision taken by each of the Gram Sabha. If the Sarpanch, or more than ten per cent of the members or fifty members of the Gram Sabha whichever is less, give requisition in writing for a special meeting of the Gram Sabha, the Secretary shall call such a meeting within seven days of the receipt of such requisition. The Secretary of the Gram Panchayat shall also be the Secretary of the Gram Sabha. The Secretary shall be under the control of the Gram Sabha and perform such duties as assigned to him by the Gram Sabha. All matters brought before any meeting of Gram Sabha shall be decided, as far as possible, unanimously, failing which by general consensus of the members present; provided that where there is difference of opinion on any issue such matter shall be brought before the next meeting. If a decision is not taken unanimously or by general consensus in successive two deferred meetings then such matter shall be decided by a majority. If any dispute arises as to whether a person is entitled to vote, the same shall be decided by the person presiding on the basis of the entry in the list of voters of the Gram Sabha area and his decision shall be final.

Functions of the Gram Sabha

The Gram Sabha shall perform the following functions: sanitation, conservancy, prevention and abatement of nuisance; construction, repair and maintenance of public wells, ponds and tanks and supply of water for domestic use; construction and maintenance of sources of water for bathing and washing and supply of water for domestic animals; construction and maintenance of village roads, culverts; bridges, bunds and other works and building of public utility; construction, maintenance and clearing of public streets, latrines, drains, tanks, wells and other public places; filling in of disused wells, unsanitary ponds, pools, ditches and pits and conversion of step wells into sanitary wells; lighting of village streets and other public places; removing of obstructions and projections in public streets and places and sites not being private property or which are open to use of public, whether such sites are vested in the panchayat or belongs to the State Government, regulating and control over entertainment shows, shops, eating houses and vendors of drinks, sweetmeats, fruits, milk and of other similar articles; regulating the construction of houses, latrines, urinals, drains and water closets; management of public land and management, extension and development of village site; regulating places for disposal of dead bodies, carcasses and other offensive matters; disposal of unclaimed corpses and carcasses; earmarking places for dumping refuse; regulation of sale and preservation of meat; maintenance of Gram Sabha property; establishment and management of cattle ponds and maintenance of records relating to cattle; maintenance of ancient and historical monuments other than those declared by or under law made by Parliament to be of national importance, grazing lands and other lands vesting in or under the control of the Gram Sabha; maintenance of records of births, deaths and marriages; rendering assistance in the census operation and in the surveys conducted by the State Government or Central Government or any other local authority lawfully constituted; rendering assistance in prevention of contagious diseases; rendering assistance in inoculation and vaccination and enforcement of other preventive measures for safety of human beings and cattle prescribed by government department concerned; rendering assistance to the disabled and destitutes; promotion of youth welfare, family welfare and sports; establishment of Raksha Samiti for safety of life and property;

prevention of fire and extinguishing fire and safety of property during outbreak of such fires; plantation and preservation of village forests; removal of social evils like dowry; granting loans for the purposes of providing medical assistance to indigent persons in serious and emergency cases; disposal of dead body of an indigent person or any member of his family; or any other purpose for the benefit of an indigent person as may be notified by the State Government from time to time subject to such terms and conditions as may be prescribed; carrying out the directions or orders given or issued by the State Government, the Collector or any other officer authorised by the State Government in this behalf with respect to the measures for amelioration of the condition of the SCs and STs and OBCs and in particular in regard to the removal of untouchability; perform such functions as may be entrusted to it by Zilla Panchayat or Janpad Panchayat by general or special orders; to exercise and perform such other powers and functions as the State Government may confer on or entrust to under this Act or any other law for the time being in force in the state; provided that where any such function is entrusted to the Gram Sabha, it shall act as an agent of the State Government, Zilla Panchayat or Janpad Panchayat, as the case may be, and necessary funds and other assistance for the purpose shall be provided to it by the State Government, Zilla Panchayat or Janpad Panchayat, as the case may be; plan and manage basic amenities; select beneficiaries under various programmes; implement, execute and supervise development schemes and construction work within the Gram Sabha area; control and monitor beneficiary oriented schemes and programmes; promote general awareness amongst the people at large; organise voluntary labour and contribution for community work and promote the concept of community ownership; to plan, own and manage minor water bodies up to a specified water area situated within its territorial jurisdiction; to lease out any minor water body up to a specified area for the purpose of fishing and other commercial purposes; to regulate the use of water of rivers, streams, minor water bodies for irrigation purposes; to exercise control over institutions and functionaries in all social sectors transferred to or appointed by the Gram Sabha.

Committees under the Gram Swaraj System

The Gram Sabha shall, for discharging its functions and duties, constitute the following standing committees: (1) Gram Vikas Samiti, (2) Sarvjanik Sampada Samiti, (3) Krishi Samiti, (4) Swasthya Samiti, (5) Gram Raksha Samiti, (6) Adhosanrachna Samiti, (7) Shiksha Samiti, and (8) Samajik Nyay Samiti.

In addition to the standing committees mentioned above, the Gram Sabha may constitute one or more such ad hoc committees, as it may deem necessary for the implementation of any time-bound work. The committee shall comprise of members who are beneficiaries of work assigned to the committee. The committee shall cease to exist after submitting the completion report and evaluation of the work by the Gram Sabha. The Committees which are already functioning within the area of jurisdiction of the Gram Sabha shall continue to function with the approval of the Gram Sabha. The number of members, reservation of seats, term of office, procedure for resignation and removal, conduct of business, eligibility for becoming a member, meeting, mode of filling of vacancies and procedure of standing committees and ad hoc committees shall be such as may be prescribed.

Every standing committee other than Gram Vikas Samiti shall have a President who shall be elected by the members of the committee from amongst themselves. The term of office of the President shall be one year, provided that the President shall be elected from amongst the members belonging to SCs, STs, OBCs, other category and from amongst women members by such rotation as may be prescribed.

The Gram Vikas Samiti shall comprise of nine members. All the Presidents of the standing committees shall be members of Gram Vikas Samiti. The President and Vice President of the Gram Vikas Samiti shall be Sarpanch and Up-sarpanch of concerned Gram Panchayat respectively. The powers, functions and duties of the committee shall be such as may be entrusted to it by the Gram Sabha from time to time. Every committee shall be responsible and accountable to the Gram Sabha and shall work under its control and supervision. The Gram Sabha shall have power to remove any member of the committee at any time for the reasons to be recorded in writing. The Gram Vikas Samiti shall prepare a plan for overall development of the village and submit it for the approval of the Gram Sabha.

Every committee other than the Gram Vikas Samiti, shall elect from amongst the members of the Gram Sabha a Secretary by two-thirds majority of members of the committee; provided that if there is a resident Jan Swasthya Rakshak in the village under the scheme of the Public Health Department of the State Government he may be appointed as Secretary of the Swasthya Samiti. Provided further that a person shall not hold charge of a Secretary if such person happens to be a relative of any member of that committee. The Secretary shall be honorary and his educational qualification shall be such as may be determined by the committee. He shall be responsible to the committee as well as to the Gram Sabha.

Every Gram Sabha shall prepare annually in such form and in such manner and by such date, as may be prescribed, budget estimates of its receipt and expenditure for the next financial year.

Elections of the Members of Standing Committees

A standing committee shall comprise of members who are stake-holders of the work assigned to it. Gram Sabha shall determine number of members of the standing committee. The number of members of each committee shall not however be more than twelve.

Meeting for the Constitution of Standing Committees

The Sarpanch of Gram Panchayat shall within one month of date of notification of the Rules, convene a meeting of the Gram Sabha for constituting the standing committees. Fifty per cent of the members of each standing committee so constituted shall belong to

SCs, STs and OBCs, two-third of which shall be from SCs, STs and remaining one-third from OBCs. The seats of the members of the standing committee, other than Gram Vikas Samiti, shall be filled by the Gram Sabha, in its meeting, in accordance with provisions laid down in the Act. Provided that in case members belonging to SCs or STs or OBCs are not available for seats so reserved, such seats shall be filled by available persons belonging to other categories and the remaining seats shall be filled in from the non-reserved class. Provided further that each standing committee shall have at least one-third women members. No person other than a Panch shall be a member of more than one standing committee at a time. Panch of the Gram Panchayat may be a member of any two standing committees other than Gram Vikas Committee.

Term of the President and Members of the Standing Committees

The term of the President of Gram Vikas Samiti who is also the Sarpanch of the Gram Panchayat shall be co-terminus with the term of the Sarpanch. Provided that in case of the office of the Sarpanch falling vacant for any reason, the Up-sarpanch shall be the President of Gram Vikas Samiti till the elected Sarpanch takes over the charge. The term of the President of the standing committees other than the Gram Vikas Samiti shall be one year. The term of the members of the standing committees excluding Gram Vikas Samiti shall be five years.

Election of President of Standing Committees

For the first time every standing committee except Gram Vikas Committee shall be held within one month after its constitution and elect a President from amongst its members. While electing the President of a standing committee for the first time, the category to which the President shall belong shall be determined by drawing of lots. After expiry of the term of the President for the first time, the election of the President for the subsequent period shall be as provided in the Act, excluding the category to which the first

President belonged in the same order as provided in the Act. The election of the President shall as far as possible be unanimous failing which, by general consensus of the members present.

Resignation, Removal and Filling up of the Office Bearers of the Standing Committees

The President of any standing committee other than the Gram Vikas Samiti may resign from the post by submitting his resignation in writing to the Sarpanch. Any member of a standing committee other than the Gram Vikas Samiti may resign by submitting his resignation in writing to the President of the standing committee. The Gram Sabha may remove any member of a committee at any time for reasons to be recorded in writing. In case of a casual vacancy of a member occurring due to death, resignation or removal of any member of the standing committee, the vacancy so caused shall be filled within one month from the same category for the remaining period of the tenure in accordance with the provision of these rules.

Powers, Functions and Duties of Standing Committees

Subject to the provisions of the Act, the standing committee shall have powers and functions and duties as may be entrusted to it by the Gram Sabha and in relation to such powers, functions and duties: call for papers, documents and other information in the same manner and to the same extent as the Gram Sabha has the power to call; prepare and submit progress reports of the schemes, programmes falling within its purview to the Gram Sabha from time to time; shall function within the policy framework laid down by the Gram Sabha; shall perform such functions as may be delegated by the State Government; shall be accountable to the Gram Sabha. The Gram Vikas Samiti shall prepare a plan for overall development of the village and submit it for approval of the Gram Sabha. The standing committee shall be assigned the subjects mentioned below in general:

- *Gram Vikas Samiti:* For all matters connected with all rural development programmes, planning, budget, account, taxation, management of the Gram Kosh and other financial matters and subjects not covered by the functions allotted to any other committee.

- *Sarvajanik Sampada Samiti:* Land, forest, water resources, mineral resources and environment.
- *Krishi Samiti:* Agriculture, animal husbandry, cooperation, reclamation including soil conservation and contour bunding and fisheries, compost manuring, seed distribution and other matters connected with the development of agriculture and livestock.
- *Swasthya Samiti:* Matters connected with the public health such as inoculation, measure for prevention of diseases, supervision of Primary Health Centres and dispensaries in the Gram Sabha area, cleanliness, water supply and drainage, etc.
- *Gram Suraksha Samiti:* All works relating to safety of life and property, relief of distress caused by flood, drought, earthquakes, etc.
- *Adhosanrachana Samiti:* Rural roads, communication, rural housing, public buildings and works, and energy, etc.
- *Shiksha Samiti:* All matters relating to primary education and literacy.
- *Samajik Nyaya Samiti:* All matters related to removal of untouchability, welfare of SCs, STs and OBCs, removal of social evils like dowry and welfare of disabled, old and destitute, women and child welfare. Any other function, which may be assigned to any committee by the Gram Sabha.

Procedure for Conduct of Business

The President of the standing committee may convene a meeting of the standing committee as often as may be necessary; The President shall convene a meeting of the standing committee on a written requisition signed by at least 50 per cent members of the committee; If a meeting is not held within 10 days of the receipt of the said requisition the Secretary of the committee shall call such meeting.

Notice of every meeting specifying the date, time and place thereof and business to be transacted there shall be given to each member by the Secretary of the committee, at least three days before the meeting. The quorum necessary for the meeting of the standing committee shall be one half of the members constituting of the standing committee including the presiding authority. If at any meeting there are not sufficient members present to form the quorum, the presiding authority shall adjourn the meeting to such time or date as he thinks fit and announce the same at once and the business which would have been brought before the original meeting had there been a quorum there at, shall be brought before the adjourned meeting and may be disposed of at such meeting or at any subsequent adjourned meeting. However, no meeting shall be held without quorum.

The President shall preside over all meetings of the standing committee but in his absence, the members present shall elect one from amongst themselves to preside over that meeting. No business other than that specified in the notice for the meeting shall be transacted at a meeting except with the previous approval of the presiding authority; where any matter concerns more than one standing committee it shall be placed for decision before the Gram Sabha; where any matter is a matter of policy, it shall be placed for decision of the Gram Sabha.

The Secretary of the standing committee shall be as provided in the Act. The Secretary of the standing committee shall attend the meeting of the standing committee unless prevented by a reasonable and sufficient cause and may tender information or clarification in respect of any matter under discussion. The Secretary of the standing committee may at any meeting of the standing committee explain or make statement in regard to any subject under discussion at such meeting. The Secretary of the standing committee shall be accountable to the standing committee and to the Gram Sabha. The Secretary of the standing committee other than the Gram Vikas Samiti may be removed by a simple majority of the members of the committee for reasons to be recorded in writing. All items of business brought before any meeting of the standing committee shall be decided on the basis of consensus of opinion among the members of the committee; Provided that in case of difference in opinion, the matter shall be referred for consideration and decision of the Gram Sabha. All decisions of the standing committee shall be recorded in a register maintained for the purpose. Minutes of each meeting of standing committee shall be drawn up in Hindi written in Devnagri script and recorded in a book to be kept for the purpose and shall be signed by the Presiding Authority of the meeting and the Secretary of the standing committee. The abstract of the decision taken and the minutes of the meeting of the standing committee shall be placed in the next meeting of the Gram Sabha. No subject once finally disposed of by the standing committee shall be reconsidered by it within a period of six months without consent of not less than three-fourths of the member of the standing committee.

In addition to the standing committees, the Gram Sabha may constitute one or more such ad hoc committees, as it may deem necessary for the implementation of any time-bound work as decided upon by the Gram Sabha. The Gram Sabha may also constitute ad hoc Committees for specific purposes, if any. The ad hoc committee shall comprise of members who are stakeholders. The ad hoc committee shall cease to exist after the submission of completion report to the Gram Sabha and evaluation of work done by such committee by the Gram Sabha unless the Gram Sabha decides otherwise. The ad hoc committee shall have such number of members as the Gram Sabha may deem fit and shall include youth and women members as far as possible. The composition and procedure of conduct of business and all other allied matters shall be as decided by the Gram Sabha. Each ad hoc committee shall elect a chairperson from amongst its members. Each ad hoc committee shall nominate a member secretary who shall, with the approval of the chairperson of the committee, convene the meeting of the committee as and when required. The member secretary shall keep a record of the proceedings of the meeting of the ad hoc committees. All decisions by the ad hoc committees shall be taken by consensus, failing which by simple majority. Each ad hoc committee shall perform such functions as assigned to it by the Gram Sabha, and shall be bound by the decision of the Gram Sabha. Each ad hoc committee shall be accountable to the Gram Sabha. A Panch may be a member of such ad hoc committee, which pertains to the Panch's constituency or in which Panch is a stakeholder. All rules corresponding to these rules and enforced immediately before the commencement of these rules are hereby repealed in respect of the matters covered by these rules. Provided that any order made or any action taken under the rules so repealed shall be deemed to have been made or taken under the corresponding provisions of these rules.

Gram Kosh

Every Gram Sabha shall establish a fund to be called the Gram Kosh consisting of following four parts: (i) Anna Kosh, (ii) Shram Kosh, (iii) Vastu Kosh, (iv) Nagad Kosh and there shall be credited thereto (a) donations, (b) income from other sources, (c) any sum received from the Gram Panchayat fund including proceeds from land revenue, cess on land revenue, grazing fees and Shala-upkar, to be allotted to the Gram Sabha according to norms fixed by the State Government, (d) taxes imposed by Gram Sabha, and (e) any sums received by Gram Panchayat under various schemes sponsored by the Central Government or the State Government, to be allotted to the Gram Sabha according to norms prescribed by the Central Government or the State Government subject to the provisions of this Act and the rules made thereunder all property vested in the Gram Sabha and the Gram Kosh shall be applied for the purposes of this Act or for other purposes connected with the activities for the development of village: Provided that funds received under any scheme shall be utilised according to the guidelines issued by the Central Government, or the State Government, as the case may be . The Gram Kosh shall be kept and maintained in such manner and in such form as may be prescribed. The Gram

Kosh shall be operated by the Gram Vikas Samiti and all amounts from the Gram Kosh shall be drawn under joint signature of the Treasurer and Secretary of the Gram Vikas Samiti with the approval of the Gram Sabha. The information regarding all receipts into and drawls from the Gram Kosh shall be placed before the Gram Sabha in its next meeting. There shall be a Treasurer of Gram Kosh who shall be nominated by the Gram Vikas Samiti in such manner as may be prescribed. The Gram Sabha shall cause to be maintained proper books of accounts and prepare annual statement of accounts. The accounts of the Gram Sabha shall be audited from time to time in such manner and by such authority as may be prescribed and the Audit Report submitted shall be placed before the next meeting of the Gram Sabha. The Gram Sabha shall have the power to withhold salary, sanction leave, inspect and supervise the work of a government employee whose area of jurisdiction lies within the limits of Gram Sabha area. Gram Sabha shall have the power to recommend to the competent authority imposition of penalties in respect of a government employee for misconduct and negligence of duties. The State Government may, by general or special order, add or withdraw functions and duties entrusted to Gram Sabha when the State Government undertakes execution of any of the functions entrusted to Gram Sabha.

Functioning of Gram Kosh

Nature of Fund: (i) Anna Kosh; (ii) Shram Kosh; (iii) Vastu Kosh; and (iv) Nagad Kosh. There shall be credited into the fund: (i) taxes imposed by the Gram Sabha; (ii) any sum received by Gram Sabha under various schemes sponsored by the Central Government or State Government; (iii) any sum received from the Gram Panchayat Fund including proceeds from land revenue, cess on land revenue, grazing fees and Shala Bhawan Upkar allotted to the Gram Sabha by the Gram Panchayat; (iv) income from other sources; and (v) donation. The Treasurer will submit monthly report of all transactions in the Anna Kosh by the 7th of the next month to the Gram Vikas Samiti.

Anna Kosh

An Anna Kosh will be established by each Gram Sabha. Each Gram Sabha will establish an Anna Kosh by collecting contribution from Bhumiswamis in the Gram Sabha area. The quantum of contribution to be collected from Bhumiswamis will be decided by the Gram Sabha. The Gram Sabha will be competent to collect contribution of grains as resources for development works. The Gram Sabha may receive donations in the form of grains. Grains returned by loanees will be deposited in the Anna Kosh.

Loan from Anna Kosh may be given to any needy person with the approval of the Gram Sabha. Limit of loan of food grain to a person can be fixed by the Gram Sabha. For doing any development work, such quantity of food grain can be withdrawn from Anna Kosh, and utilised up to such extent which may be determined by the Gram Sabha. In any emergency situation a maximum quantity of 50 kilograms of grain may be sanctioned for withdrawal by the President of Gram Vikas Samiti, in anticipation of the approval of Gram Sabha.

The grains deposited in the Anna Kosh will remain under the safe custody of the Treasurer who will ensure that the grains are stored with due diligence. The Treasurer will maintain monthly and annual account. Minimum balance in Anna Kosh will be maintained as determined by Gram Sabha from time to time. All loans from the Anna Kosh will be recovered in such number of instalments as the Gram Sabha may determine. The Gram Sabha may also levy interest at a reasonable rate, which can be recovered, in the form of grain or cash. The Gram Sabha may after recording reasons in writing, write-off such loans and damaged stock if any, as it may deem fit. The Treasurer will maintain a loan and recovery register in the Form 1A. The Treasurer will submit monthly/annual accounts of loans and recoveries to the Gram Vikas Samiti. Monthly/annual accounts of the Anna Kosh will indicate the value in rupees equivalent of monthly/annual transactions. For calculating the value in Rupee equivalent, local price of grains will be considered.

Shram Kosh

Gram Sabha may raise additional resources by organising voluntary labour. Gram Sabha will register all such persons who are willing to contribute voluntary labour for development work of the village. Gram Sabha will ensure that there is no forced labour or engagement of child labour. Each Gram Sabha will maintain the accounts of Shram Kosh in Form 2. For all such works in which the villagers contribute voluntary labour, work-wise detail of number of persons contributing, number of days, etc., will be calculated. The Treasurer will submit monthly/annual accounts to the Gram Vikas Samiti. Monetary equivalent of all such voluntary labour will be calculated for which the minimum wage rate will be used for such calculation.

Vastu Kosh

Each Gram Sabha will establish a Vastu Kosh. The Gram Sabha may receive any items from the villagers or from any other sources. The accounts of all receipts into the Vastu Kosh will be maintained in Form 3. The monetary value of each item received into the Vastu Kosh will be shown by taking local value of the material. Any item from the Vastu Kosh will be utilised, used or other wise disposed off with the approval of Gram Sabha. The Vastu Kosh may also receive temporary receipts such as tractors, trollies, irrigation tubewells and other equipment for temporary use of the Village Committee.

Nagad Kosh

The Gram Sabha shall in accordance with the instructions issued by the State Government from time to time, keep the Nagad Kosh in a savings account in any nationalised bank, co-operative bank, or post office. Gram Vikas Samiti with the approval of the Gram Sabha shall nominate a treasurer from amongst members of the Gram Sabha. The post of the Treasurer shall be honorary. The minimum educational qualification for the Treasurer shall be 10th class pass. The Treasurer may be removed by the Gram Vikas Samiti with the approval of the Gram Sabha. Every Gram Sabha shall maintain the registers in Form 4 (rules for receipt and expenditure in the manner prescribed in these rules). Before the use of register, they shall be bounded and the pages shall be serially numbered. Any correction made in the register shall be countersigned by the Treasurer. No amount payable to Gram Sabha shall be allowed to remain due without adequate reasons. In case any such amount does not seem to be recoverable, it shall be adjusted, remitted, reduced or written-off with the sanction of Gram Sabha. All amounts shall be withdrawn by cheques. Any amount from the Nagad Kosh shall not be withdrawn unless it is required for immediate use. The maximum amount to be withdrawn in one transaction shall be such as may be decided by the Gram Vikas Samiti. Unspent balance, if any, not exceeding Rs 500 may be kept with the Treasurer of Gram Vikas Samiti for such maximum period as may be decided by the Gram Sabha and it shall be deposited in the Nagad Kosh if not spent within the said period. All withdrawals shall be made under the joint signature of Treasurer and the Secretary of the Gram Vikas Samiti. The President of Gram Vikas Samiti shall ensure that the total expenditure does not exceed the sanctioned budgeted amount and that the allotted amount is spent on the items budgeted for. All amount received by the Gram Sabha shall be deposited in the Savings Account immediately, not later than three days by the Treasurer. All payments to other parties shall be made by cheques issued to the person concerned to receive such payment directly from the bank or post office, as the case may be. Small expenditure like day-to-day expenditure shall be met out from the permanent imprest, the limit of which may be fixed by the Gram Vikas Samiti. All cash transactions shall be entered in the account register in Form 4 and shall be countersigned by the Treasurer. The account book shall be closed daily and shall be signed by the Treasurer. In the end of every month, the balance of the account book shall be verified by the President of Gram Vikas Samiti and the following certificate shall be given with the signature and date of the President: "Certified that the cash balance has been checked and found correct". In case of cash payments by the tax-payers or other persons, a receipt in Form 5 shall be given to the payer. The receipt in Form 5 shall be issued after the amount is actually credited to the Gram Kosh if the payment is received by cheque. All claims for payment shall be presented in a Bill form to the Treasurer of the Gram Sabha and scrutinised and sanctioned by the President of Gram Vikas Samiti. All rules corresponding to these rules and enforced immediately before the commencement of these rules are hereby repealed in respect of the matters covered by these rules. Provided that any order made or any action taken under the rules so repealed shall be deemed to have been made or taken under the corresponding provisions of these rules.

Schedule I-A

Obligatory Taxes to be imposed by Gram Sabha

1. A property tax on the lands or buildings or both, the capital value of which including the value of the land is more than Rs. 6,000 other than (a) the buildings and lands owned or vested in the Union or State Government, Gram Sabha, Gram Panchayat, Janpad Panchayat, or Zilla Panchayat: (b) the buildings and lands or portions thereof used exclusively for religious or educational purposes including boarding houses.
2. A tax on private latrines payable by the occupier or owner of the buildings to which such latrines are attached when cleaned by Gram Sabha agency.
3. A light tax, if light arrangements have been made by the Gram Sabha.
4. A tax on person, exercising any profession or carrying on any trade falling within the limits of Gram Sabha area.

Schedule II-A

Other Optional Taxes, Fees etc. to be imposed by Gram Sabha

1. A tax on building not covered under Item 1 in Schedule 1-A.

2. A tax on animals used for riding, driving, draught or burden or on dogs or pigs payable by the owners thereof.
3. Fees for the use of sarais, dharamshalas, rest houses, slaughterhouses and encamping grounds.
4. A water rate where arrangements are made by the Gram Sabha for regular supply of water.
5. A tax on persons carrying on the profession of purchaser, agent, commission agent, weighman, or a measurer within the meaning of Madhya Pradesh Krishi Upaj Mandi Adhiniyam, 1972 (No. 24 of 1973), in the area of Gram Sabha excluding the area of a Mandi.
6. A temporary tax for special works of public utility.
7. A tax for the construction or maintenance of public latrines and a general scavenging tax for removal and disposal of refuses.
8. Fees for bullock-cart stand and tonga stand.
9. Fees for temporary structure or any projection over any public place or temporary occupation thereof.
10. Fees for grazing cattle over the grazing grounds vested in the Gram Sabha.
11. Any other tax, which the State Legislature has power to impose under the Constitution of India.

The Provisions of the Madhya Pradesh Panchayat Raj (Sanasodhan) Adhiniyam, 2001 shall not apply to the Scheduled areas so far as they are inconsistent with the provisions of Chapter XIV A of the Act and the provisions of "The Provisions of the Panchayats (Extension to the Scheduled Areas) Act, 1996 (No. 40 of 1996)".

An appeal against the decision of a Gram Sabha shall lie to a committee consisting of the President of Janpad Panchayat, a member of Janpad Panchayat of that area and the Sub-Divisional Officer (Revenue) in such manner as may be prescribed.

3

The Study Design

Madhya Pradesh was the first state that not only made legislation as per the 73rd Amendment Act and organised elections to the panchayats and constituted also the institutions of local self-governance. The panchayats in Madhya Pradesh completed their first five-year term in 1999 and the second round of panchayat elections was held in 2000. The third round of election was held in 2005. Madhya Pradesh has responded proactively to its first initial years' experience and amended, on the basis of that rich experience, the Madhya Pradesh Panchayat Act to make significant changes by introducing the system of Gram Swaraj.

The Madhya Pradesh Panchayat Raj Act drastically altered the existing governance system and constitutionalised grassroots democracy. The government realised that Panchayat Raj Institutions (PRIs) working as agents of change have altered rural society and still has the potential to transform it further. Thus, Madhya Pradesh, a pioneer in the implementation of the Panchayat Raj Act, presents a good case study on the basis of which larger trends and implications for decentralised rural self-governance can be identified from the point of view of innovation of Gram Swaraj.

This study is an attempt to document the processes of change in Madhya Pradesh, which led to the establishment of Gram Swaraj, and also to fully comprehend and analyse the implications of the making it as the pivot of grassroots democracy.

In this backdrop the study is an attempt to find out all the pros and cons of the working of Gram Swaraj and its implications for the totality of the Panchayat Raj. The study is designed to seek the answers of basic questions like: What is the level of participation of people, including women in Gram Sabha? How are decisions taken in Gram Sabha? How do the various committees function? How far the role of Sarpanch has changed? How the change in the system has been perceived by the people in villages?

Objectives

The objectives of the study are as follows:

- To find out awareness and perceptions of people about Gram Swaraj.
- To assess the level of awareness and perceptions of Panchayat Raj representatives about Gram Swaraj.
- To know the level of participation of people in Gram Sabha.
- To evaluate the role performance of various committees.
- To find out the practical problems in implementation of Gram Swaraj.
- To suggest viable measures for the betterment of Gram Swaraj.

Area and Focus of Study

The main focus of this research was the Gram Sabha within the Panchayat Raj system. The panchayat representatives, native elites, local bureaucracy and Gram Sabha members have been considered within the study, so as to comprehend the dynamics of its working, change and development. The study also planned to understand the interplay, inter-linkages and conflict between these actors. Study focused on the conditions for the implementation of Gram Swaraj and its implications on the PRIs in particular and governance space in Madhya Pradesh in general.

Research Questions

The following are the guiding questions of the research:

- How have the rural citizens responded to this new change?
- How is this new change going to ascertain better participation in Gram Sabha than under the previous system of Panchayat Raj as witnessed?
- How are the issues of quorum and participation of weaker section of society looked after?
- How are the stakeholders chosen for various committees and how are the committees working (agenda/meeting/decision)?
- How are these committee decisions discussed and analysed in Gram Sabha meetings and how are they implemented?
- How far has this change ensured the 'say' of have-nots at grassroots level?
- What are the factors and imponderables involved in the working of Gram Swaraj and how are these challenges managed?
- How do the traditional socio-economic elites of villages react to this new paradigm?
- How is the grassroots leadership involved with the dispensation of new system?
- What are the dark areas of the new system and how to remove them?

Methodology

Universe of Study

The major concern of the project is to study the experiment of Gram Swaraj in Madhya Pradesh. Two districts of the state are selected purposively for the micro-level study. The selected districts are Shajapur and Dewas. The basic reason for the selection of these districts was fair representation of all sections of society in the population.

Sampling Frame

The study, an evaluative one in nature is fact based, descriptive and analytical. A proportionate sampling framework has been adopted.

The obvious advantage of proportionate sampling is that it ensures a proper representation of attributes or variables, which are considered most significant for the study.

Sampling Procedure

For a proper special coverage one block was selected from each selected district. The selection of a block was based on the fair representation of SC, ST and OBC population in the block. From the selected blocks, five Gram Panchayats were selected where due representation was given to women-headed Gram Panchayats. Thus, from two districts, two blocks were selected and 10 Gram Panchayats were chosen for the study.

Units of Observation and Sample Size

Gram Sabha members, committee chairpersons/members and panchayat representatives secretaries were the units of observation.

Table 3.1

Sampling Design: Panchayat Raj Representatives

Name of Village	*Sarpanch*	*Up-Sarpanch*	*Panch*	*Panchayat Secretary*	*Total*
Shajapur (District)					
Shajapur (Block)					
Sentkhedi	01	01	03	01	06
Piplya Gopal	01	01	03	01	06
Siroliya	01	01	03	01	06
Shihoda	01	01	03	01	06
Abhaypur	01	01	03	01	06
Dewas (District)					
Sonkatch (Block)					
Chaubarajagir	01	01	03	01	06
Dudlai	01	01	03	01	06
Phavda	01	01	03	01	06
Agera	01	01	03	01	06
Lalakhedi	01	01	03	01	06
Total	10	10	30	10	60

From each selected Gram Panchayat – 6 Gram Sabha Members, (3 male and 3 female), 5 Standing Committee Chairpersons/ Members, 5 Panchayat Representatives (1-Sarpanch, 1-Up-sarpanch and 3-Panch), 1 Koshadhyaksha and 1 Panchayat Secretary was taken for an interview. Thus from each selected block – 30 Gram Sabha Members, (15 male and 15 female), 25 Standing Committee Chairpersons/Members, 25 Panchayat Representatives (5-Sarpanch, 5-Up-sarpanch and 15-Panch), 5 Koshadhyakshas and 5 Panchayat Secretaries were selected. In all, from 2 blocks of two districts the size of sample was 60 Gram Sabha Members, 120 Standing Committee Chairpersons/ Members, Panchayat Representatives, *Koshadhyaksha* and Panchayat Secretary. The total size of sample was 180.

Table 3.2

Sampling Design: Gram Sabha Members

Name of Village	*Gram Sabha Member*		*Standing Committee President/Member*	*Treasurer*	*Total*
	Female	*Male*			
Shajapur (District)					
Shajapur (Block)					
Sentkhedi	03	03	05	01	12
Piplya Gopal	03	03	05	01	12
Siroliya	03	03	05	01	12
Shihoda	03	03	05	01	12
Abhaypur	03	03	05	01	12
Dewas (District)					
Sonkatch (Block)					
Chaubarajagir	03	03	05	01	12
Dudlai	03	03	05	01	12
Phavda	03	03	05	01	12
Agera	03	03	05	01	12
Lalakhedi	03	03	05	01	12
Total	30	30	50	10	120

Data Collection

Primary and secondary data were collected for the study. Secondary data were based on books, journals, monographs, occasional papers, government publications, circular, orders, ordinances, etc.

For primary data two separate interview schedules were structured and administered among the respondents (Gram Sabha members, panchayat representatives, committee chairpersons, *koshadhyaksha* and panchayat secretaries). The interview schedules were broadly divided into two parts. Part first dealt with awareness and exposure of the respondents towards Gram Swaraj. Second part gave emphasis on perceptions about impact of Gram Swaraj. Each interview schedule had 45-50 questions. An interview schedule took almost one hour to fill up. The research team under the strict supervision of Project Director interviewed the respondents personally. Besides this, in each selected village, a village-listing schedule was administered among all the households of the village and secondary data related to Gram Sabha meeting and village data were also gathered from Gram Panchayat office.

It was also considered important to make use of observational method to seek information and get insight into the issues involved. A diary was maintained to record the observations throughout the fieldwork. These observations supplemented the writing of ground realities section of the report.

Data Processing

The study was mainly based on primary data. On the basis of collected data a codebook was prepared. All the interview schedules were coded accordingly. Coded schedules were entered in the computer. SPSS (version 10) package was used for analysis and interpretation of data.

4

Profile of Selected Villages

Present study is based on primary data. For the purpose of data collection and to understand the grassroots reality, 10 villages were selected for an in-depth survey. Two separate interview schedules were administered one for Panchayat Raj representatives and another for Gram Sabha members. Besides these, a village listing schedule and a questionnaire were also administered to know the profile of the villages, meetings of Gram Sabhas, participation of people and other similar issues. Village-wise details are given hereunder:

Siroliya (Shajapur)

The village is situated 14 km inside the Agra-Mumbai national highway. The distance of the village from district headquarters is 18 km. The approach road is kachcha and stony. The village is not accessible by road. Ujjain-Guna railway line passes through this village.

According to 2001 Census, the population of the village is 2,188 (1,142 males and 1,046 females). Out of this, 37.1 per cent are SCs and 7.1 per cent are STs. the literacy rate of the village is 83.8 per cent. Major occupation of the villagers is agriculture, followed by agriculture labour. Average size of household is five.

Siroliya has one secondary and one primary school and an 'Anganwadi' centre. Drinking water is a problem in the village. Because of the factor of untouchability the supply of water through community water tank is restricted to upper caste people. The village is electrified. Every family in the village has a house. For marketing, villagers depend on the nearby town Maxi (14 km away).

Gram Panchayat Siroliya has 20 members. Sarpanch is a woman from OBC category. Her husband is very influential and does all work on her behalf. Caste category-wise representation of voters in Gram Sabha is as follows: 43 per cent SCs, 52 per cent OBCs and 5 per cent general.

Since the inception of Gram Swaraj on 26 January 2001, 21 meetings of Gram Sabha have taken place. But, due to lack of quorum, maximum meetings could not be operationalised. In the meetings, matters related to development are discussed and forwarded for further action.

All the eight standing committees are formed in the village. Due procedure was followed in the formation of committees and adequate representation was provided to all the committees as per the rules. Committee meetings have also taken place, though not as per the given schedule.

Piplya Gopal (Shajapur)

The village is situated inside the Shajapur-Bercha road. The distance of the village from the district headquarters is 8 km. The approach road is 3 kilometres long and is kachcha. Villagers have their own mode of transportation and public transport is also available from the main road.

According to 2001 Census, the population of the village is 1,325 (694 males and 631 females). Out of this, 35.5 per cent are SCs. The literacy rate of the village is 53.4 per cent. Major occupation of the villagers is agriculture, followed by agriculture labour. Average size of household is six.

The village has equal population of Hindu and Muslim communities. There are three dominant caste groups, namely,

Pathans, Harijans and Patidars. Schooling facility is confined to middle school and an 'Anganwadi' centre. Drinking water is adequately available in the village. The village is totally electrified and streetlights are also provided. All the drainage and kharnja (stone/brick road) work is in working order. Every family in the village has a house. For market, villagers depend on nearby town of Shajapur (8 km away).

Gram Panchayat Piplya Gopal consists of 19 members. Sarpanch is a man from SC category. Category-wise representation of voters in Gram Sabha is as follows: 39 per cent SCs, 22 per cent OBCs and 39 per cent general.

Since inception of Gram Swaraj on 26 January 2001, 29 meetings of Gram Sabha have taken place. But due to lack of quorum maximum meetings could not be operationalised and only four meetings were successfully convened. In meetings matters related to development are discussed and forwarded for further implementation. Besides this, prohibition of liquor and issue of Padhna-Badhana Andolan have also been included in the agenda of meetings.

All the eight standing committees are formed in the village and one special committee on water resources is also formed. Due procedure was followed in the formation of committees and adequate representation was provided to all the committees as per the provisions of the Act. Except for one committee, meetings have also taken place as prescribed.

Abhaypur (Shajapur)

The village is situated on the Agra-Mumbai national highway. The distance of the village from the district headquarters is 14 km. Villagers have their own mode of transportation and public transport is also frequently available.

According to 2001 Census, the population of the village is 2,822 (1,535 male and 1,287 female). Out of this, 42.9 per cent are SCs and 2.2 per cent are STs. The literacy rate of the village is 78 per cent. Major occupation of the villagers is agriculture labour, followed by agriculture. Average size of household is six.

Village has dominance of Patidar community. They are agriculturists and well-off financially whereas the SC community depends mostly on agriculture labour in the village or in nearby towns. As far as schooling facility is concerned, the village has one high school, one middle school and two primary schools. Besides these, one 'Anganwadi' centre and one private school is also operational. Drinking water is adequately available in the village. The village is totally electrified and streetlights are also provided. All the drainage and kharnja work are in working order. Every family in the village has a house. Villagers usually get most of the things of daily use in the village but for market needs they go to the nearby town of Panwadi (2 km away).

Gram Panchayat Abhaypur has 20 members in the Gram Panchayat. Sarpanch is a male from OBC category. Caste-wise representation of voters in Gram Sabha is as follows: 47 per cent SCs, 44 per cent OBCs, 3 per cent STs and 6 per cent general.

Since inception of Gram Swaraj on 26 January 2001, 10 meetings of Gram Sabha have taken place and others could not be convened due to lack of quorum. In meetings, matters related to development like selection of beneficiaries, inclusion of name in BPL list are discussed and forwarded for further implementation.

All the eight standing committees are formed in the village and one special committee on water resources is also formed. Due procedure was followed in the formation of committees and adequate representation was provided to all the committees as prescribed. Committee meetings have rarely taken place and when held, they were not as per the given schedule.

Shihoda (Shajapur)

The village is situated on the Shajapur-Nainawad road. The distance of the village from the district headquarters is 18 km. Village is located four km inside from the Nainavad. The approach road is kachcha and stony. Some public transport is available in the village itself.

According to 2001 Census, the population of the village is 1,033 (537 males and 496 females). Out of this, 42.7 per cent are

SCs. The literacy rate of the village is 79.5 per cent. Major occupation of the villagers is agriculture, followed by agriculture labour. Average size of household is six.

Village has a good mixture of all communities. General community is dominated by Rajputs. OBC community has a fair representation of Jats. As far as schooling facility is concerned, the village has one middle school and one primary school. Besides these, one 'Anganwadi' centre is also operational. Drinking water is adequately available in the village. The village is totally electrified but no streetlights are provided. Every family in the village has a house. For market, villagers are dependent on nearby towns Shajapur (18 km away), Maxi (15 km away) and Banjari (4 km away).

Shihoda has 20 members in Gram Panchayat. Sarpanch is a woman from OBC category. The Gram Panchayat covers two villages and Sarpanch is from the other village. The villagers argue that women Sarpanch's husband takes all the responsibility of Sarpanch and all development works are confined to their village. Category-wise representation of voters in Gram Sabha is as follows: 17 per cent SCs, 23 per cent OBCs and 60 per cent general.

Since inception of Gram Swaraj on 26 January 2001, 27 meetings of Gram Sabha have taken place and others could not be convened due to lack of quorum. In meetings, many development works are discussed and forwarded for further implementation like eradication of water problem, construction works, selection of beneficiaries, inclusion of name in BPL list, etc. Besides these, efforts were also made to minimise the differences among different communities.

All the eight standing committees are formed in the Gram Sabha. Due procedure was followed in the formation of committees and adequate representation was provided to all the communities. Committee meetings have also taken place though not as per the given schedule. In all the respective meetings of committees, issues were discussed threadbare and recommendations were placed before the Gram Sabha.

Sentkhedi (Shajapur)

The village is situated on the Shajapur-Bercha road. The distance of the village from district headquarters is 8 km. The village is located 3 km inside from the main road. The approach road is kachcha. Some public transport is available in the village itself but usually villagers go to main road to get public transport.

According to 2001 Census, the population of the village is 2,822 (1,535 males and 1,287 females). Out of this, 42.9 per cent are SCs and 2.1 per cent are STs. The literacy rate of the village is 78 per cent. Major occupation of the villagers is agriculture labour, followed by agriculture. Average size of household is six.

The village has dominance of Gurjar community. A sizeable number is from SC community. As far as schooling facility is concerned, the village has only one primary school and an 'Anganwadi' centre. Drinking water is adequately available in the village. The village is totally electrified and but no streetlights are provided. Every family in the village has a house. For market, villagers depend on nearby town Bercha (8 km away).

Gram Panchayat Sentkhedi has 11 members in the Gram Panchayat. Sarpanch is a male from OBC category. Dominance of a particular caste in the village promotes a situation where decisions are taken by a few; thus decision-making is undemocratic which is resented by the villagers. Caste-wise representation of voters in Gram Sabha is as follows 40 per cent SCs, 55 per cent OBCs and 5 per cent general.

Since inception of Gram Swaraj on 26 January 2001, 11 meetings of Gram Sabha have taken place and others could not be convened due to lack of quorum. In meetings, matters related to development like selection of beneficiaries for different schemes, construction works, inclusion of name in BPL list are discussed and forwarded for further implementation.

All the eight standing committees are formed in the village. Due procedure was followed in the formation of committees and adequate representation was provided to all the committees as per the prescribed procedure. Committee meetings have also taken place and when held were not as per the given schedule and number. In all the respective meetings of committees, issues were discussed threadbare and recommendations were submitted in Gram Sabha meetings.

Chaubarajagir (Dewas)

The distance of the village from district headquarters is 45 km. The village is located inside the main road. The approach road is kachcha and of four km. Village is not accessible through road. The public transport is almost negligible in the village. The approach road is under construction.

According to 2001 Census, the population of the village is 2,543 (1,364 males and 1,179 females). Out of this, 30.8 per cent are SCs and 3 per cent are STs. The literacy rate of the village is 54.1 per cent. Major occupation of the villagers is agriculture, followed by agriculture labour. Average size of household is six.

The village has a mix population of Hindu and Muslim. The village is located near a huge pond and irrigation of the land is done through it. It has one middle school and an 'Anganwadi' centre. Drinking water is adequately available in the village. The village is electrified. Every family in the village has a house. For market villagers are dependent on nearby town Sonkatch (9 km away).

Gram Panchayat Chaubarajagir has 22 members in the Gram Panchayat. Sarpanch is a male from general category. Category-wise representation of voters in Gram Sabha is as follows: 30 per cent SCs, 42 per cent OBCs, 3 per cent STs and 25 per cent general.

Since inception of Gram Swaraj on 26 January 2001, 22 meetings of Gram Sabha have taken place. But due to lack of quorum maximum meetings could not be operationalised. In meetings, many development works are discussed and forwarded for further action like inclusion of name in BPL list, selection of beneficiaries, encroachment, sanitary campaign, drainage, kharanja, etc.

All the eight standing committees are formed in the village. Due procedure was followed in the formation of committees and adequate representation of all communities provided to all the committees as per the procedure. Committee meetings have also taken place though not as per the given schedule and number.

Dudlai (Dewas)

The village is situated on the inner side of the Indore-Bhopal road. The distance of the village from district headquarters is 35 km. The approach road is one km. Villagers have their own mode of transportation and public transport is available from the village.

According to 2001 Census, the population of the village is 1,039 (528 males and 511 females). Out of this, 26.1 per cent are SCs and 1.3 per cent are STs. The literacy rate of the village is 69.7 per cent. Major occupation of the villagers is agriculture, followed by agriculture labour. Average size of household is six.

Village population is dominated by OBCs. Schooling facility is confined to middle school and an 'Anganwadi' centre. Besides these, one private school is also there. Drinking water is adequately available in the village. The village is totally electrified and streetlights are also provided. Every family in the village has a house. For market, villagers depend on nearby town Sonkatch (3 km away) and Gandhavapuri (3 km away).

Gram Panchayat Dudlai has 10 members in the Gram Panchayat. Sarpanch is a male from OBC category. Category-wise representation of voters in Gram Sabha is as follows: 26 per cent SCs, 72 per cent OBCs, 1 per cent STs and 1 per cent general.

Since inception of Gram Swaraj on 26 January 2001, 30 meetings of Gram Sabha have taken place. In meetings, matters related to development like distribution of ration card, selection of beneficiaries, inclusion of name in BPL list, etc., are discussed and forwarded for further implementation. Besides this, the issue of prohibition of social evils has also been in the agenda of meetings.

All the eight standing committees are formed in the village and one special committee on water resources is also formed. Due procedure was followed in the formation of committees and adequate representation was provided to all the committees as per the procedure, though committee meetings could not be convened as per the given schedule.

Phavda (Dewas)

The village is situated on the Indore-Bhopal highway. The distance of the village from district headquarters is 23 km. Villagers have their own mode of transportation and public transport is frequently available.

According to 2001 Census, the population of the village is 1,236 (628 males and 608 females). Out of this, 9.7 per cent are SCs and 1.6 per cent is STs. The literacy rate of the village is 59.4 per cent. Major occupation of the villagers is agriculture labour, followed by agriculture. Average size of household is six.

Village has a mixture of all communities. Since the village is located on roadside, major working groups depend on labour in the village while others work in nearby towns for livelihood. As far as schooling facility is concerned, the village has one high school, one middle school and two primary schools. Besides these, one 'Anganwadi' centre and one private school is also here. Drinking water is adequately available in the village. The village is totally electrified and streetlights are also provided. All the drainage and kharnja work are done. Every family in the village has a house. Villagers get usually most of their articles of daily use in the village itself but for market, if needed, they go to nearby town of Dewas (23 km away) and Sonkatch (5 km away).

Gram Panchayat Phavada has 20 members in the Gram Panchayat. Sarpanch is a woman from SC category. Category-wise representation of voters in Gram Sabha is as follows: 9 per cent SCs, 44 per cent OBCs, 1 per cent STs and 46 per cent general.

Since inception of Gram Swaraj on 26 January 2001, 10 meetings of Gram Sabha have taken place and others could not be convened due to quorum. In meetings, matters related to development like selection of beneficiaries, inclusion of name in BPL list, etc., are discussed and forwarded for further implementation.

All the eight standing committees are formed in the village and one special committee on water resources is also formed. Due procedure was followed in the formation of committees and adequate representation was provided to all the committees as per the procedure. Committee meetings have rarely taken place and whenever convened, given schedule was not followed.

Agera (Dewas)

The village is situated six km away from the block headquarters. The distance of the village from district headquarters is 37 km. The village is located three km inside from the main road. The approach road is pucca. Some public transport is available in village itself and villagers have their own mode of transportation.

According to 2001 Census, the population of the village is 1,530 (776 males and 754 females). Out of this, 30.4 per cent are SCs and 16.7 per cent are STs. The literacy rate of the village is 60.5 per cent. Major occupation of the villagers is agriculture labour, followed by agriculture. Average size of household is six.

Village has a good mixture of all communities. General community is dominated by Rajputs. As far as schooling facility is concerned, the village has one middle school and one primary school. Besides these, one private school is also here. Drinking water is adequately available in the village. The village is totally electrified and streetlights are also provided. Every family in the village has a house. For market, villagers depend on nearby town of Sonkatch (6 km away).

Gram Panchayat Agera has 19 members. Sarpanch is a male from general category. Category-wise representation of voters in Gram Sabha is as follows: 30 per cent SCs, 9 per cent STs, 33 per cent OBCs and 28 per cent general.

Since inception of Gram Swaraj on 26 January 2001, 31 meetings of Gram Sabha have taken place but only 11 meetings could be convened due to quorum. In meetings, matter related to development like inclusion of name in BPL list, construction works, selection of beneficiaries, etc., are discussed and forwarded for further implementation.

All the eight standing committees are formed in the village. Due procedure was followed in the formation of committees and adequate representation was provided to all the committees as per the procedure. Committee meetings have also taken place though not as per the given schedule.

Lalakhedi (Dewas)

The village is situated three km away from the main road. The distance of the village from district headquarters is 38 km. The approach road is kachcha. Some public transport is available in village itself but usually villagers go to main road to get the public transport.

According to 2001 Census, the population of the village is 678 (360 males and 318 females). Out of this, 19 per cent are SC. The literacy rate of the village is 63 per cent. Major occupation of the villagers is agriculture followed by agriculture labour. Average size of household is six.

Village has dominance of Rajput community. As far schooling facility is concerned, the village has a middle, a primary school and an 'Anganwadi' centre. Drinking water is adequately available in the village. The village is totally electrified. Every family in the village has a house. For market, villagers depend on nearby town Sonkatch (7 km away).

Gram Panchayat Lalakhedi has 20 members in the Gram Panchayat, out of them 10 are from Lalakhedi. Sarpanch is a woman from general category. Dominance of Rajput caste in the village promotes a situation where decisions are taken by a few persons and democratic decision-making is not followed, so believe the villagers. Category-wise representation of voters in Gram Sabha is as follows: 26 per cent SCs, 11 per cent OBCs and 63 per cent general.

Since inception of Gram Swaraj on 26 January 2001, 31 meetings of Gram Sabha have taken place and but only six meetings could be convened due to quorum. In meetings, matters related to development like selection of beneficiaries for different schemes, construction works, inclusion of name in BPL list and many development works are discussed and forwarded for further implementation.

All the eight standing committees are formed in the village. Due procedure was followed in the formation of committees and adequate representation was provided to all the committees as per the procedure. Committee meetings have also taken place though not as per the given schedule. In all the respective meetings of committees, issues were discussed threadbare and recommendations were submitted in Gram Sabha meetings.

Villagers' Participation in Panchayat Activity

After discussing village profile, a brief elaboration of the issues like background of panchayat, attending Gram Sabha and visitors in Gram Sabha are discussed. The data are based on a village-listing schedule administered amongst villagers during the survey. The responses could be gathered only from those families that were available at home during the survey.

Table 4.1

Representation of Family in Panchayat

Village	*Yes*	*No*	*Total*
Dewas			
Chaubarajagir	04 (4.9)	81(95.1)	85 (100.0)
Agera	10 (12.4)	71 (87.6)	81 (100.0)
Lalakhedi	02 (3.3)	58(96.7)	60 (100.0)
Dudlai	05 (7.3)	63 (92.7)	68 (100.0)
Phawda	07 (7.2)	90 (92.8)	97 (100.0)
Shajapur			
Abhaypur	10 (11.8)	75 (88.2)	85 (100.0)
Sihoda	16 (23.5)	52 (76.5)	68 (100.0)
Sirolia	16 (18.8)	69 (81.2)	85 (100.0)
Sentkhedi	06 (11.8)	45 (88.2)	51 (100.0)
Piplya Gopal	10 (19.6)	41 (80.4)	51 (100.0)
Total	86 (11.8)	645 (88.2)	731 (100.0)

Figures in parentheses are percentages.

Table 4.1 elaborates the background of the household from the point of view of representation of the family in panchayat in 10 selected villages. The question was asked to 731 households. Only 11.8 per cent households in the villages have a background of panchayat representatives, whereas 88.2 per cent households were never associated with the panchayat either as elected or nominated members. This percentage in both the districts varies in a significant manner. Dewas district has a very limited representation of households in panchayat, whereas Shajapur district has this representation in a considerably high number. This broad-based representation of households in panchayat is a step forward in the direction of better participation and involvement in panchayat activities.

Table 4.2

Participation in Gram Sabha Meetings

Village	*Regular*	*Seldom*	*Never*	*Total*
Dewas				
Chaubarajagir	02 (2.4)	26 (30.6)	57 (67.0)	85 (100.0)
Agera	05 (6.2)	16 (19.8)	60 (74.0)	81 (100.0)
Lalakhedi	07 (11.7)	16 (26.7)	37 (61.6)	60 (100.0)
Dudlai	02 (2.9)	10 (14.7)	56 (82.4)	68 (100.0)
Phawda	05 (5.1)	22 (22.7)	70 (72.2)	97 (100.0)
Shajapur				
Abhaypur	01 (1.2)	21 (24.7)	63 (74.1)	85 (100.0)
Sihoda	05 (7.4)	15 (22.0)	48 (70.6)	68 (100.0)
Sirolia	10 (11.8)	39 (45.9)	36 (42.3)	85 (100.0)
Setkhedi	02 (3.9)	10 (19.6)	39 (76.5)	51 (100.0)
Piplya Gopal	02 (3.9)	17 (33.3)	32 (62.8)	51 (100.0)
Total	41 (5.6)	192 (26.3)	498 (68.1)	731 (100.0)

Figures in parentheses are percentages.

Thus, it is clear from the above analysis that the households represented in panchayats vary from village to village. However, the average representation ratio is high and if the rotatory system of representation allows maximum households to represent the panchayat, the system would throw up a seasoned, experienced and informed lot of members in the village.

The revival of Gram Sabha has been an issue of serious concern for the State Government. It is known for certain that to make the Gram Sabha vibrant and hub of all activities, Gram Swaraj system was introduced. With this perception in mind, households of selected villages were asked about their participation in Gram Sabha meetings.

Table 4.3

Attending Gram Sabha Meetings

Village	*All (Men and Women)*	*Only Men*	*Head of the Family*	*Nobody Attend*	*Total*
Dewas					
Chaubarajagir	00 (0.0)	26 (30.6)	01 (1.2)	58 (68.2)	85 (100.0)
Agera	04 (4.9)	15 (18.5)	00 (0.0)	69 (76.5)	81 (100.0)
Lalakhedi	01 (1.7)	21 (35.0)	01 (1.7)	37 (56.9)	60 (100.0)
Dudlai	03 (4.4)	09 (13.2)	00 (0.0)	56 (82.3)	68 (100.0)
Phavda	01 (1.0)	24 (24.7)	00 (0.0)	72 (74.2)	97 (100.0)
Shajapur					
Abhaypur	00 (0.0)	22 (25.9)	00 (0.0)	63 (74.1)	85 (100.0)
Sihoda	00 (0.0)	19 (27.9)	00 (0.0)	49 (72.0)	68 (100.0)
Sirolia	08 (9.4)	29 (34.1)	13 (15.3)	35 (11.2)	85 (100.0)
Sentkhedi	00 (0.0)	12 (23.5)	00 (0.0)	39 (76.5)	51 (100.0)
Piplya Gopal	01 (1.9	18 (35.3)	00 (0.0)	32 (62.8)	51 (100.0)
Total	18 (2.5)	195 (26.7)	15 (2.1)	503 (68.7)	731 (100.0)

Figures in parentheses are percentages.

Out of 731 households only 5.6 per cent reported that they regularly participate in Gram Sabha meetings whereas 26.3 per cent responded that they seldom attended the meetings. Remaining 68.1 per cent household pointed out that they never participated in the meetings.

Since the required quorum for the Gram Sabha meeting is one-fifth of the total member, the requisite number is maintained with great difficulty; in fact a very minuscule number in every village attends the meetings regularly while a considerably high number never attend meetings. It is surprising to note this apathy of the villagers, particularly when the panchayats and Gram Sabhas have been given most of the powers to make them units of self-governance. The feedback that we got from our respondents was that many of them are unaware of the amendment package.

It has been argued that all the members do not attend Gram Sabha. Usually men or specific group of them go to attend the Gram Sabha meeting. Looking into this dynamics, it was asked to the households that from their family who attend the Gram Sabha meeting. Out of 731 households, only 2.5 per cent households are of the view that all men and women attend the meetings of Gram Sabha. Around 26.7 per cent household point out that only men of the family attend the Gram Sabha meetings. Only 2.1 per cent household argue that head of family attend Gram Sabha meeting. Remaining 68.7 per cent household are of the view that nobody attends the meetings. It is clear from the above analysis that in majority cases nobody attends the meeting whereas a significant number opine that only men attend the meetings. Despite having a statutory provision of one-third representation of women is mandatory for the quorum of Gram Sabha meeting, a clear-cut apathy is discernible among the households.

5

Panchayat Raj Representatives' Participation, Attitudes and Perceptions towards Gram Swaraj: An Analysis

Gram Swaraj has emerged as a new system of local self-governance at the village level in Madhya Pradesh which has moved from indirect to direct democracy. It is based on the premise that in a village people can assemble and sit together to discuss and settle local issues and therefore representatives are not required to represent aspirations and interests of the people. The new system intends to give power directly to the people rather than their representatives. To operationalise this system in the field, it has been decided to strengthen the Gram Sabha, which under the new structure is authorised to exercise all the powers of Gram Panchayats and many more powers. Gram Sabhas are expected to function as decision-making bodies of the local people for local affairs.

While visualising the new system, the framers of Gram Swaraj were completely aware and conscious of the hierarchical social order and inequitable power relations in the village; therefore to protect Gram Swaraj from becoming a handmaid fiefdom of the privileged few, certain provisions have been inserted as safeguards to protect the interests of the larger community in general and deprived categories in particular. The architects of the new system asserted that the quorum of a Gram Sabha should not be less than one-fifth of the total number of members of the Gram Sabha. Importantly, of these, not less than one-third should be women, and the SCs and STs shall be represented in proportion to their population in the Gram Sabha. This clearly indicates that a generic quota for the deprived, which could otherwise be short-circuited, has been discarded and a more stringent safeguard to ensure the participation of deprived communities has been built in.

Another progressive innovation of the new Gram Swaraj system is to organise separate Gram Sabhas for each village. In Madhya Pradesh a Gram Panchayat is often constituted of more than one village. To do justice to each village and to make the system of Gram Swaraj effective it was imperative to recognise the Gram Sabha of each village as an independent local body.

Gram Swaraj has emerged from an extensive process of deliberation, refinement and dialogue. It is also a result of the grassroots experiences of Panchayat Raj functioning coupled with Madhya Pradesh government's stated commitment to democratic decentralisation. The primary objective of introducing the new system of Gram Swaraj is evidently to transfer power to the people and sincerely to take forward the process of democratic decentralisation to its logical end. The new structure is substantially influenced by the Gandhian commitment to Gram Swaraj to facilitate social, economic and political autonomy at the village level.

Against this backdrop, the study is designed to investigate the functioning of Gram Swaraj as well as to fully understand the attitudes and perceptions of the Panchayat Raj representatives, the operators of the system. A structured interview schedule was administered for this purpose. Besides this, informal discussions and field observations were also of help to provide inputs to strengthen the arguments in analysis. This chapter analyses in detail the various facets of Gram Swaraj from the point of view of Panchayat Raj representatives.

Caste

After the 73rd Amendment Act, due representation has been given to all the castes to participate in the panchayat affairs. Through Gram Swaraj, it has been ascertained that particularly the weaker and marginalised sections of the society are duly represented in the decision-making process of the Gram Sabha. In Madhya Pradesh, provisions have been made to give due representation to SCs, STs, OBCs and women in panchayats.

Table 5.1
Caste

Caste	*Number of Respondents*	*Percentage*
General	15	25.0
SC	13	21.7
ST	01	01.7
OBC	31	51.7
Total	60	100.0

Keeping in view the provisions of the new Act, Panchayat Raj representatives were chosen from different castes and communities for the study. Table 5.1 shows that 51.7 per cent respondents are from OBC category and 25 per cent respondents represent the general group. Remaining 21.7 per cent respondents are from Scheduled Caste (SC) category whereas one respondent is from ST category. Thus, it is clear from the above analysis that all the categories in the selected village population are properly represented in the sample.

Age

Age is one of the important aspects concerned to the present study. It shows the background of experience of the respondents that comes with age. For purposes of analysis, age has been categorised in three groups as 21 to 35, 36 to 50 and 51 and above.

Table 5.2 reveals that 53.3 per cent of the respondents fall in the age group of 36 to 50 and 31.7 per cent respondents are from the age group of 21 to 35, whereas the rest 15 per cent respondents belong to the age group of 51 and above. It clearly demonstrates that the majority of the respondents is below the age of 50.

Table 5.2
Age

Age	*Number of Respondents*	*Percentage*
21 to 35	19	31.7
36 to 50	32	53.3
51 and above	09	15.0
Total	60	100.0

Sex

Sex is a very important indicator in analysing socio-economic characteristics of the respondents. It is also assumed that the levels of exposure, awareness and points of views of both the sexes are different, particularly in rural scenario. Thus the factor of sex has been kept in view while constructing the sample.

Table 5.3
Sex

Sex	*Number of Respondents*	*Percentage*
Male	48	80.0
Female	12	20.0
Total	60	100.0

Table 5.3 indicates that 80 per cent respondents are male whereas the representation of female is 20 per cent. Since one-third representation of female is made mandatory in the panchayats, efforts were made to get one-third women in the sample but somehow only 20 per cent respondents could be taken due to the unavailability of women members in adequate number in the field during survey.

Education

Education is also one of the basic indices to assess the socio-economic status of an individual. Since independence, efforts have been made to provide educational facilities to all sections of society. A certain minimum level of literacy is the basic requirement for the people to get out of the trap of ignorance and backwardness. Despite all efforts to enhance the levels of literacy, the scenario is still disappointing in the rural area particularly for the marginalised sections and for women.

Table 5.4
Education

Education	*Number of Respondents*	*Percentage*
Illiterate	08	13.3
Literate	13	21.7
Primary	11	18.3
Secondary	10	16.7
Higher Secondary	12	20.0
Graduate and above	06	10.0
Total	60	100.0

Table 5.4 reflects that 21.7 per cent respondents are just literate and 20 per cent respondents are educated up to higher secondary level, with 18.3 per cent respondents educated up to primary level. Around 16.7 per cent respondents are educated up to secondary level and 10 per cent respondents are graduates and above. Remaining 13.3 per cent respondents are illiterate. Thus, it is clear from the analysis that majority of the respondents are educated up to a desired level of literacy. Looking into the rural background of respondents wherein one-fifth are female, it appears that the educational level is considerably very good.

Occupation

Occupation is one of the very important indices to analyse the background of the respondents. In rural India, the occupation of the majority of the population is either agriculture or labour.

Table 5.5 shows that 73.3 per cent respondents are engaged in agriculture work, 15 per cent respondents are housewives and 5 per cent respondents are equally engaged to labour and service. Remaining 1.7 per cent respondents do business work. Thus, it has clearly emerged out that majority of the respondents do agriculture work. A significant number (15%) of respondents are housewives.

Table 5.5
Occupation

Occupation	*Number of Respondents*	*Percentage*
Agriculture	44	73.3
Labour	03	05.0
Business	01	01.7
Service	03	05.0
Housewife	09	15.0
Total	60	100.0

Candidature for Panchayat

Village society in India is a close society where selection of a candidate for elections is usually determined by a variety of considerations. The nomination is usually decided by the villagers in many cases, whereas caste and socio-economic elites also have their role as well. Of late political parties too have penetrated in local elections to establish their hegemony in decision-making process of the local candidates.

Table 5.6
How the Candidature Was Decided

Candidature	*Number of Respondents*	*Percentage*
By villagers	45	75.0
By political parties	02	03.3
By rural elites	04	06.7
Self-interest	07	11.7
By caste people	02	03.3
Total	60	100.0

Table 5.6 reflects the agencies that decided candidature for panchayat election. Whereas 75 per cent respondents are of the view that the village community decided their candidature, 11.7 per cent respondents point out that it was their own decision. In the opinion of 6.7 per cent respondents, rural elites have decided the candidature and 3.3 per cent respondents equally argue that political parties and caste people have decided the candidature. It is evident from the above analysis that three-fourths of the respondents are of the view that the candidature is decided by villagers; it is indeed a pointer that village community has a hand in deciding as who would represent the village in its elective body.

Panchayat Election

Table 5.7 provides the details of election, wherein 65 per cent respondents assert that they contested and won the election of their own with 33.3 per cent respondents of the view that the election was unanimous/unopposed. Only one respondent argues that the election was on the basis of caste. It is indeed a matter of satisfaction that two-thirds respondents have come to the panchayat through the election route, whereas one-third were elected unopposed.

Table 5.7
How was the Election?

Election	*Number of Respondents*	*Percentage*
Unanimous/unopposed	20	33.3
By winning election	39	65.0
Basis of caste	01	01.7
Total	60	100.0

Pre-experience of Working in Panchayat

Table 5.8 shows whether the respondents had any earlier experience of working in panchayats. Only 28.3 per cent respondents have previous experience of working in panchayats, whereas remaining 71.7 per cent respondents do not have any previous experience of working in panchayats. Thus, it is clear from the above analysis that in majority of the cases the respondents do have previous experience of the working in panchayat.

Table 5.8

Any Earlier Experience of Working in Panchayat

Any Earlier Experience	*Number of Respondents*	*Percentage*
Yes	17	28.3
No	43	71.7
Total	60	100.0

Out of 17 respondents who had previous experience of working in panchayat, Table 5.9 indicates the posts they held. In all 14 respondents point out that they were Panch, whereas remaining three respondents, one each was Janpad Panchayat member, Up-sarpanch and Sarpanch.

Table 5.9

If Yes, Post

Post	*Number of Respondents*	*Percentage*
Panch	14	82.3
Janpad Panchayat member	01	05.9
Up-sarpanch	01	05.9
Sarpanch	01	05.9
Total	17	100.0

Regularity of Panchayat Meeting

Gram Panchayat meeting should take place every month. Table 5.10 illustrates the information related to panchayat meeting. As much as 83.3 per cent respondents feel that panchayat meetings do take place regularly, whereas remaining 11.7 per cent respondents point out that the panchayat meetings are not held regularly. It is interesting to note that overwhelming majority of the respondents feel the meetings are regular.

Table 5.10

Does the Panchayat Meeting take place Regularly?

Regularity of Panchayat Meeting	*Number of Respondents*	*Percentage*
Yes	53	88.3
No	07	11.7
Total	60	100.0

Table 5.11 interprets the reasons for non-regularity of panchayat meetings. Out of seven respondents who have argued that the meetings are not regular, three respondents point out the reason that as they do not get information. Two respondents feel that there is unavailability of panchayat building. One respondent gives the reason "Sarpanch is not interested". Remaining one respondent does not know the reason of his absence. Thus, it is clear from the analysis that the respondents have pointed out some specific reasons for the irregularity of panchayat meetings.

Table 5.11

If No, Reasons

Reason	*Number of Respondents*	*Percentage*
Sarpanch in not interested	01	14.3
Due to unavailability of panchayat building	02	28.6
No information	03	42.8
Don't know	01	14.3
Total	07	100.0

Participation in Panchayat Meeting

It is very important and pertinent to know the participation of respondents in panchayat meetings. Table 5.12 illustrates respondents' point of view regarding attending meetings. With 73.3 per cent respondents reporting that they do attend panchayat meetings, it is a positive indication that almost three-fourths of the respondents attend the meetings regularly.

Table 5.12

Do you attend Panchayat Meeting Regularly?

Attending Panchayat Meeting	*Number of Respondents*	*Percentage*
Yes	44	73.3
No	16	26.7
Total	60	100.0

Table 5.13 elaborates the reasons for not attending the panchayat meetings regularly. Out of 16 respondents who have said that they do not go regularly in the meetings, seven respondents point out that they do not get timely information; six respondents argue that due to work they do not go; two of them do not understand panchayat functioning and one respondent complains that nobody listens to him. Thus, respondents have come out with a variety of reasons for not attending panchayat meeting, the principle reason being lack of information about the meeting to be held.

Table 5.13

If No, Reasons

Reason	*Number of Respondents*	*Percentage*
Don't understand panchayat functioning	02	12.5
No information	07	43.7
Nobody listens	01	06.3
Due to work	06	37.5
Total	16	100.0

Role in Panchayat Meeting

Table 5.14 explains the role of respondents in panchayat meetings. As much as 71.7 per cent respondents are of the view that they discuss issues and 18.3 per cent respondents go there merely to put their signatures, whereas 10 per cent respondents sit silently. It is clear from the above illustration that majority of the respondents participate in discussions about panchayat issues. Almost one-fourth respondents sit as idle watchers. However, it is an inciting feature that nearly 72 per cent of the respondents participate in panchayat proceedings.

Table 5.14

What is Your Role in Panchayat Meeting?

Role	*Number of Respondents*	*Percentage*
Sit silently	06	10.0
Only put signature	11	18.3
Discuss issues	43	71.7
Total	60	100.0

Visit to Various Places

Panchayat representatives have multi-faceted tasks to perform in panchayats. It involves various jobs including visiting various offices for different purposes.

Table 5.15

Do You Visit other Offices for Panchayat Work?

Visit	*Yes*	*No*	*Total*
Tehsil	31 (51.7)	29 (48.3)	60 (100.0)
Janpad Panchayat	34 (56.7)	26 (43.3)	60 (100.0)
Zilla Panchayat	17 (28.3)	43 (71.7)	60 (100.0)
Collector's Office	11 (18.3)	49 (81.7)	60 (100.0)
Court	01 (01.7)	59 (98.3)	60 (100.0)
State Capital	04 (06.7)	56 (93.3)	60 (100.0)

Figures in parentheses are percentages.

Table 5.15 explains the information related with visit to different places. In response to the question whether they visit different places for panchayat work, the place-wise response is as follows: Tehsil is visited by 51.7 per cent respondents. Janpad Panchayat is visited by 56.7 per cent respondents. Zilla Panchayat is visited by 28.3 per cent respondents. Collector's office is visited by

18.3 per cent respondents. State capital and court are visited by 6.7 per cent and 1.7 per cent respondents respectively.

Table 5.16

If Yes, Reasons

Reason	*Number of Respondents*	*Percentage*
Tehsil		
For meetings	01	03.2
For personal work	04	13.0
For villagers problem	15	48.3
For panchayat work	11	35.5
Total	31	100.0
Janpad Panchayat		
For villagers problem	14	41.2
For personal work	03	08.8
For meetings	05	14.7
For Indira Awaas	01	02.9
For government work	11	32.4
Total	34	100.0
Zilla Panchayat		
For villager's problem	08	47.0
For government work	05	29.5
For meetings	04	23.5
Total	17	100.0
Collector's Office		
For villager's problem	06	54.6
For personal work	01	09.0
For government work	04	36.4
Total	11	100.0
Court		
For government work	01	100.0
Total	01	100.0
State Capital		
For personal work	04	100.0
Total	04	100.0

Thus, it is very clear from the responses that half of the respondents visit Tehsil and Janpad Panchayat. A considerable number of them visit Zilla Panchayat. Other offices of little or no importance are visited by a very few numbers. This exposure of respondents clearly demonstrates that the Sarpanch, secretary and some other representatives visit the offices for panchayat work.

Table 5.16 interprets the reasons for visiting various offices. According to respondents who visited various places have reasons to visit specific places. The place-wise reasons of visit are listed below: Tehsil visit: for meetings (1), for personal work (4), for villagers' problems (15), for panchayat work (11). Janpad Panchayat visit: for villagers' problems (14), for personal work (3), for meetings (5), for Indira Awaas (1), for government work (11). Zilla Panchayat visit: for villagers' problems (8), for government work (5), for meetings (4). Collector's office visit: for villagers' problem (6), for personal work (1), for government work (4). Court visit: for government work (1). State capital visit: for personal work (4).

Thus, it is evident from the above analysis that the visits are mostly done for village problems, panchayat work or official work. Though the number is limited but it is important that they are fully conversant with the functional and operational aspects of panchayat system.

Exposure towards Important Individuals

Table 5.17 highlights the approach of respondents to such individuals who are directly related to panchayat activities. The purpose behind having this question is to know whom the panchayat representative knows better and how important he is in panchayat functioning. An MP is known to 20 per cent respondents, Minister-in-Charge is known to 53.3 per cent respondents, an MLA is known to 76.7 per cent respondents, Zilla Panchayat chairperson is known to 55 per cent respondents, Janpad Panchayat chairperson is known to 66.7 per cent respondents, Collector is known to 11.7 per cent respondents, Zilla Panchayat, CEO is known to 35 per cent respondents, Janpad Panchayat, CEO is known to 46.7 per cent respondents, Tehsildar is known to 58.3

per cent respondents, police inspector is known to 51.7 per cent respondents, bank manager is known to 66.7 per cent respondents, and doctor is known to 63.3 per cent respondents.

Table 5.17

Do you know Important Individuals?

Individual	*Yes*	*No*	*Total*
Member of Parliament	12 (20.0)	48 (80.0)	60 (100.0)
Minister-in-Charge	32 (53.3)	28 (46.7)	60 (100.0)
MLA	46 (76.7)	14 (23.3)	60 (100.0)
Zilla Panchayat Chairperson	33 (55.0)	27 (45.0)	60 (100.0)
Janpad Panchayat Chairperson	40 (66.7)	20 (33.3)	60 (100.0)
Collector	07 (11.7)	53 (88.3)	60 (100.0)
CEO, Zilla Panchayat	21 (35.0)	39 (65.0)	60 (100.0)
CEO, Janpad Panchayat	28 (46.7)	32 (53.3)	60 (100.0)
Tehsildar	35 (58.3)	25 (41.7)	60 (100.0)
Police Inspector	31 (51.7)	29 (48.3)	60 (100.0)
Bank Manager	40 (66.7)	20 (33.3)	60 (100.0)
Doctor	38 (63.3)	22 (36.7)	60 (100.0)

Figures in parentheses are percentages.

Thus, it is clear from the above analysis that MLA is the most known person. Chairpersons of Zilla and Janpad Panchayats and Minister-in-Charge are also known to a significant number. Since these persons are directly involved in helping panchayats for various works, the local leadership has to have knowledge of such important persons related to panchayats in one way or the other. Collector, who was the most powerful name for decades in independent India, is the least known name now for local leadership.

Panchayat Work through Individual Effort

Table 5.18 makes an attempt to know whether the respondents have made any attempt for any work of panchayat. According to 48.3 per cent respondents, they have made attempt to do the work of panchayat, whereas 51.7 per cent respondents have not made any such attempt. It is indeed a matter of concern that only less than half of the respondents have made personal efforts for panchayat work.

Table 5.18

Have You done any Work for Panchayat Through Your Own Effort?

Work Done through Individual Effort	*Number of Respondents*	*Percentage*
Yes	29	48.3
No	31	51.7
Total	60	100.0

Table 5.19 illustrates the nature of work for which efforts were made by the respondents. Out of 29 respondents, four are of the view that they make efforts for work related to basic activities. As many as 16 respondents point out that their efforts are for construction work and two respondents feel that their efforts are for education related issues. Six respondents clarify that the efforts are for watershed-related activities. Only one respondent replies that his effort is to help villagers. It makes very clear that responses to the question is of mixed nature. In fact, if any issue is raised in Gram Sabha meeting, the issue has to be discussed threadbare and then some appropriate proposal is forwarded through Janpad Panchayat to Zilla Panchayat for quick disposal of work. It is therefore very necessary to know the role of the panchayat representatives in the execution of panchayat plans.

Table 5.19

If Yes, Nature of Work

Nature of Work	*Number of Respondents*	*Percentage*
Work related to basic activities	04	13.8
Work related to construction	16	55.2
Education related	02	06.9
Watershed related	06	20.7
Help to villagers	01	03.4
Total	29	100.0

Selection of Beneficiaries

Table 5.20 describes the procedure adopted for the selection of beneficiaries of welfare schemes. As much as 71.7 per cent respondents are of the view that the beneficiary selection is done through Gram Sabha and 25 per cent respondents point out that the selection is done by Sarpanch/Secretary. Remaining 3.3 per cent respondents do not know about the selection procedure. It is very encouraging to know that selection of beneficiaries, who are indeed the persons for whom such schemes have been introduced, is done as per the rules. However, one-fourth respondents still feel that Sarpanch/Secretary violates the rule in identifying the needy person.

Table 5.20

How the Beneficiaries are Selected for Welfare Schemes

Beneficiary Selection	*Number of Respondents*	*Percentage*
By Sarpanch/Secretary	15	25.0
Through Gram Sabha	43	71.7
Don't know	02	03.3
Total	60	100.0

Gram Sabha

The legislative empowerment of the Gram Sabha in India is a political development of utmost importance because it marks the clearest break from the most dominant political orthodoxy of this century. In Madhya Pradesh, special efforts have been made to empower the Gram Sabha.

Table 5.21

Does Gram Sabha Meeting take place Regularly?

Gram Sabha Meeting	*Number of Respondents*	*Percentage*
Yes	57	95.0
No	03	05.0
Total	60	100.0

Table 5.21 loudly speaks that 95 per cent respondents believe that there are regular meetings of Gram Sabha. Only 5 per cent respondents do not feel so. It is indeed a matter of satisfaction that 95 per cent respondents point out regularity of Gram Sabha meetings; this is of much significance for the successful working of Gram Swaraj system in Madhya Pradesh.

Table 5.22

If No, Reasons

Reason	*Number of Respondents*	*Percentage*
No Quorum	5	100
Total	5	100

Out of five respondents, who were of the view that the Gram Sabha meetings do not take place regularly, Table 5.22 explains that all the five respondents are of the view that meetings are not regularly possible due to lack of quorum.

Gram Sabha Quorum

After introduction of Gram Swaraj in Madhya Pradesh, an Amendment in the State Act has been made with respect to quorum. The basic assumption for the change was to have a proper and mandatory representation of all sections of society.

Table 5.23

Required Quorum for Gram Sabha Meeting

Quorum Required	*Number of Respondents*	*Percentage*
Right	38	63.3
Wrong	22	36.7
Total	60	100.0

The quorum required for the meeting is one-fifth members of the adults who have their names in the voting list of the village. Table 5.23 illustrates that 63.3 per cent respondents do know the required number of quorum whereas 36.7 per cent respondents do not know to the exact number required for quorum. It is interesting to note that almost two-thirds of the respondents know this factual information. It is also important to mention here that previously the required quorum was only one-tenths members and the previous experience was that even this number was not attainable at times. In spite of this fact, known to the government, quorum for Gram Swaraj meetings has been enhanced which is now creating difficulties in holding meetings.

Women for Gram Sabha Quorum

Women participation through 73rd Constitution Amendment Act is a landmark decision through which 33 per cent of the seats are reserved for women. This mandatory reservation is being continued for the quorum in Gram Sabha meetings as well.

Table 5.24

Do you Know that Presence of Women is Necessary for Quorum of Gram Sabha Meeting?

Women's Presence	*Number of Respondents*	*Percentage*
Yes	55	91.7
No	05	08.3
Total	60	100.0

Table 5.24 describes that 91.7 per cent respondents know that women's presence is necessary for quorum of Gram Sabha meeting. This overwhelming percentage is clearly showing that the local leadership is well aware of the fact that women's presence is required for quorum of Gram Sabha meetings.

Table 5.25

Required Number of Women for Quorum of Gram Sabha Meeting

Women for Quorum	*Number of Respondents*	*Percentage*
Right	34	61.8
Wrong	21	38.2
Total	55	100.0

The required quorum for Gram Sabha meeting is one-fifth of the total members in voter list of the village and out of them minimum one-third is needed for Gram Sabha quorum. Out of 55 respondents, 34 know the exact number of women required for the quorum. It is a positive indication that this significant aspect of mandatory women participation is known to nearly 62 per cent of the respondents.

SCs/STs for Gram Sabha Quorum

After Gram Swaraj, representation of SCs/STs in Gram Sabha meetings is made mandatory in proportion to their population. Table 5.26 shows that 91.7 per cent respondents know that the SCs/STs presence is required for quorum. Thus, it is clear from the analysis that an overwhelming majority of the respondents (91.7%) know this basic fact.

Table 5.26

Do you Know that Presence of SCs/STs is Necessary for Quorum of Gram Sabha Meeting?

Presence of SCs/STs	*Number of Respondents*	*Percentage*
Yes	55	91.7
No	05	08.3
Total	60	100.0

Participation in Gram Sabha

Gram Sabha has always been an integral part of the concept of a Gram Swaraj. Gram Sabha has been visualised as a watchdog coming between politician-bureaucratic nexus and the public at large. The important dimension of Gram Swaraj is the level of participation of people in the empowered Gram Sabha.

Table 5.27 highlights the fact that 66.7 per cent respondents participate regularly in the Gram Sabha meetings whereas 26.7 per cent respondents seldom participate in the meetings. Nearly 6.7 per cent respondents never participate in the meetings. Thus, it is evident from the above analysis that a significant percentage of respondents regularly participate in the meetings. Only a very small number never participated in the Gram Sabha meetings.

Table 5.27

Do you Participate in Gram Sabha Meetings?

Participation	*Number of Respondents*	*Percentage*
Regular	40	66.7
Seldom	16	26.7
Never	04	06.7
Total	60	100.0

Table 5.28

Reasons for Non-Participation

Reason	*Number of Respondents*	*Percentage*
Nobody listens poor/women	05	25.0
Personal business/work	08	40.0
Lack of information	06	30.0
No woman participate	01	05.0
Total	20	100.0

As many as 20 respondents are of the view that they seldom/never attend the Gram Sabha meetings and therefore it is asked as to what are the reasons of their non-participation. Table 5.28 analyses that out of 20 respondents, eight are of the opinion that their non-participation is due to their extraordinary personal busy schedule and six respondents feel that they do not get information of the meetings with five respondents regretting that their non-participation is because nobody listens to us (the poor and the women folk). One respondent feels that no woman participates for a variety of reasons. Thus, it is clear from the above analysis that the major reasons shown by the respondents are their extraordinary busy schedule, not getting information and that nobody listens to them in the meetings.

Training for Gram Swaraj

Gram Swaraj, an innovative model, as propounded by Mahatma Gandhi, has been made an integral part of Panchayat Raj system of Madhya Pradesh. This innovation has special significance from the point of view of people's participation since it has provided ample opportunities to all shades of people of the village community for direct participation in the process of decision-making. Looking into the dynamics of this new phenomenon, it is assumed that training has an important role to play to train and sensitise people for this new task. It was therefore inquired from the respondents whether they have any training for the operationalisation of the new model.

Table 5.29

Have you Received any Training Related to Gram Swaraj?

Category	*Number of Respondents*	*Percentage*
Yes	18	30.0
No	42	70.0
Total	60	100.0

Table 5.29 illustrates that only 30 per cent respondents have got training related to Gram Swaraj, whereas remaining 70 per cent respondents did not get any such training. It shows that training, an essential tool of equipping the people with capacity to run panchayat affairs, has not been carried out to make the panchayat representatives aware about the importance of Gram Swaraj and the procedural aspects of Gram Swaraj.

Table 5.30 indicates the places where training for the villagers was organised. Out of 18 respondents, 11 respondents have received such training at district headquarters, three at block headquarters and two of them equally at Commissioner's headquarters and state capital. Thus, it is clear from the analysis that respondents have received training mainly from district or block headquarters.

Table 5.30
If Yes, Where?

Place	*Number of Respondents*	*Percentage*
District headquarters	11	61.1
Block headquarters	03	16.7
Commissioner headquarters	02	11.1
State capital	02	11.1
Total	18	100.0

Table 5.31
What was the Training?

Nature of Training	*Number of Respondents*	*Percentage*
Information about rules	04	22.2
Gram Swaraj system briefed	06	33.4
Partiality should be avoided	01	05.5
Informed about rights	01	05.5
Information about records	06	33.4
Total	18	100.0

Table 5.31 provides the details of the training received by the participants. Out of the 18 respondents who received the training, six respondents were of the view that in the training, Gram Swaraj system was briefed to them. Another six respondents pointed out that information about records was given and four respondents clarified that information about rules was given. One respondent was of the critical view that there was some partiality in training which should be avoided for the sake of the new system. The remaining single respondent argued that information about rights of the Panchayat Raj representatives was given to them. Thus, it is clear from the analysis that the respondents have mainly received information/knowledge about the basics of Gram Swaraj through training.

Issues of Discussion in Gram Sabha Meetings

Gram Sabha, after the inauguration of Gram Swaraj, has been empowered to take all decisions for the multifaceted development of the village. Table 5.32 reflects the issues of discussion in Gram Sabha meetings. Nearly 31.7 per cent respondents point out that developmental issues are discussed in Gram Sabha meetings, 11.7 per cent of them feel that selection of beneficiaries is discussed, 13.3 per cent opine that village problems are discussed whereas 33.3 per cent of them report they discuss all the above-mentioned three issues. Ten per cent respondents point out that they do not know the issues of discussion. It is clear from the above presentation that local problems are the focus of discussion.

Table 5.32

What are the Main Issues of Discussion in Gram Sabha?

Main Issues of Discussion	*Number of Respondents*	*Percentage*
Related to development	19	31.7
Selection of beneficiaries	07	11.7
Related to village problems	08	13.3
About all	20	33.3
Don't know	06	10.0
Total	60	100.0

Decision-making Process

It is indeed a matter of serious concern as how decisions are taken in the Gram Sabha meetings. Table 5.33 is illustrative of the mode of decision-making process. A good 73.3 per cent respondents are of the opinion that decisions are taken unanimously and 20 per cent respondents point out that the decisions are taken as per the wish of Sarpanch. Nearly 3.3 per cent respondents do not know about the decision-making process whereas 1 respondent each points out that decisions are taken under the directions of government officials and as per the need of the village. It is clear from the above analysis that almost three-fourth respondents confirm that decisions are arrived at unanimously in panchayat meetings. It confirms that slowly and gradually people are getting involved in the process of decision-making about the issues of panchayats.

Table 5.33

How Decisions are Taken?

Decision Taking	*Number of Respondents*	*Percentage*
By Sarpanch	12	20.0
Unanimously	44	73.3
According to government officials	01	01.7
As per the need of village	01	01.7
Don't know	02	03.3
Total	60	100.0

It is very important and pertinent to know whether the villagers do contact panchayat representatives. Table 5.34 illustrates this aspect whether villagers contact with panchayat representatives. Whereas 75 per cent respondents are of the view that villagers do contact them the remaining 25 per cent respondents feel that they do not contact panchayat representatives. It is a positive indication that three-fourth respondents are contacted by the villagers for their problems, personal or public.

Table 5.34

Do Villagers Contact you?

Contact	*Number of Respondents*	*Percentage*
Yes	45	75.0
No	15	25.0
Total	60	100.0

Table 5.35 searches reasons for which villagers contact panchayat representatives. Out of 45 respondents, 23 respondents agree that the villagers do contact them for village problems. With 18 respondents pointing out that they contact for personal work

the remaining four respondents feel that they contact for developmental work. It is an established practice of local democracies that general public approaches their representatives for help/solution of their public problems. Such a practice is taking roots in Indian villages under Gram Swaraj experiment.

Table 5.35

If yes, Reasons

Reason	*Number of Respondents*	*Percentage*
For personal work	18	40.0
For village problems	23	51.1
For development work	04	08.9
Total	45	100.0

Problems Existing in Village

Table 5.36 highlights the problems in the village. Here, an effort was made to make a comparison of the problems before and after the introduction of Gram Swaraj. School was a problem for 25 per cent respondents before Gram Swaraj and it remained for 15 per cent respondents after Gram Swaraj. Health was a problem for 41.7 per cent respondents before Gram Swaraj and it increased to 43.3 per cent after Gram Swaraj. Approach road was a problem for 33.3 per cent respondents before Gram Swaraj and it remained for 30 per cent respondents after Gram Swaraj. Agriculture was a problem for none before and after Gram Swaraj. Animal husbandry was a problem for 10 per cent respondents before Gram Swaraj and it remained for 10 per cent respondents after Gram Swaraj. Labour work was a problem for 3.3 per cent respondents before Gram Swaraj and it remained for 1.7 per cent respondents after Gram Swaraj. Personal/public disputes were a problem for 1.7 per cent respondents before Gram Swaraj and it remained for 1.7 per cent respondents after Gram Swaraj. Social issues were a problem for none before and after Gram Swaraj.

Table 5.36

Problems at Village Level

Problem	*Before Gram Swaraj*		*After Gram Swaraj*	
	Yes	*No*	*Yes*	*No*
School	15 (25.0)	45 (75.0)	9 (15.0)	51 (85.0)
Health	25 (41.7)	35 (58.3)	26 (43.3)	34 (56.7)
Approach road	20 (33.3)	40 (66.7)	18 (30.0)	42 (70.0)
Drinking water	03 (05.0)	57 (95.0)	01 (01.7)	59 (98.3)
Agriculture	-	60 (100.0)	-	60 (100.0)
Animal husbandry	06 (10.0)	54 (90.0)	06 (10.0)	54 (90.0)
Labour work	02 (03.3)	58 (96.7)	01 (01.7)	59 (98.3)
Disputes	01 (01.7)	59 (98.3)	01 (01.7)	59 (98.3)
Social problem	-	60 (100.0)	-	60 (100.0)

Figures in parentheses are percentages.

Thus, it is clear from the above analysis that in most of the cases either the problems have decreased after Gram Swaraj or remained the same. Health problem has certainly remained the major problem of the village as it increased over after the establishment of Gram Swaraj.

Here the solutions are discussed in both the cases of before and after Gram Swaraj:

School Solution (Before Gram Swaraj): The solutions are as given: apprised minister in-charge (4), efforts made at Janpad Panchayat (3), proposal put before Gram Sabha (3), proposal forwarded to Zilla Panchayat (1), go to nearest village/city (4).

School Solution (After Gram Swaraj): The solutions are as given: approached minister in-charge (1), efforts made at Janpad Panchayat (3), proposal put before Gram Panchayat (1), proposal forwarded to Zilla Panchayat (2), nothing happened (3), go to nearest village/city (2).

Health Solution (Before Gram Swaraj): The solutions are as given: approached Sarpanch (1), application sent to Janpad Panchayat (2), go to nearest village/city (22).

Health Solution (After Gram Swaraj): The solutions are as given: told to MLA (1), application sent to Janpad Panchayat (2), go to nearest village/city (25).

Approach road Solution (Before Gram Swaraj): The solutions are as given: proposal forwarded in Gram Sabha (4), application sent to Janpad Panchayat (1), told to MLA (3), told to MP (1), constructed through volunteer/labour (4), told to Collector (1), nothing done (6).

Approach road Solution (After Gram Swaraj): The solutions are as given: proposal forwarded in Gram Sabha (3), proposal sent to Zilla Panchayat (2), told to MLA, nothing done (8).

Drinking Water Solution (Before Gram Swaraj): The solutions are as given: bring it from Dam (1), no progress (1), handpump on outskirt (1).

Drinking Water Solution (After Gram Swaraj): The solutions are as given: handpump on outskirt (1).

Animal Husbandry Solution (Before Gram Swaraj): The solutions are as given: go to near village/city (1).

Animal Husbandry Solution (After Gram Swaraj): The solutions are as given: go to near village/city (6).

Labour Work Solution (Before Gram Swaraj): The solutions are as given: nothing done (1), go to near village/city (6).

Labour Work Solution (After Gram Swaraj): The solutions are as given: nothing done (1).

Disputes Solution (Before Gram Swaraj): The solutions are as given: go to near village/city (1).

Disputes Solution (After Gram Swaraj): The solutions are as given: go to near village/city (1).

After discussing all the solutions for different problems before and after Gram Swaraj, it is clear that the solution procedure remained more or less the same. It can be so because, first, the new system has a very little span of time and second, the issues are of the nature that they cannot be solved within the given situation and resources.

Meeting Important Individuals

Table 5.37 explains the details regarding the individuals whom respondents met for panchayat work and for how many times. Meeting with Janpad CEO – up to 4 times (16.7%), 5 to 10 (6.7%), 11 to 15 (1.7%), no meetings (50%), many times (25%). Meeting with Janpad Chairperson – up to 4 times (15%), 5 to 10 (3.4%), 16 and above (1.7%), no meetings (48.3%), many times (30%). Meeting with Zilla Panchayat CEO – up to 4 times (15%), 5 to 10 (5.1%), no meetings (68.3%), many times (11.7%). Meeting with Zilla Panchayat Chairperson – up to 4 times (8.3%), 5 to 10 (3.4%), 16 and above (1.7%), no meetings (70%), many times (16.7%). Meeting with Collector – up to 4 times (8.3%), no meetings (88.3%), many times (3.3%). Meeting with MLA – up to 4 times (13.3%), 5 to 10 (10%), 11 to 15 (1.7%), 16 and above (1.7%), no meetings (43.3%), many times (30%). Meeting with Minister-in-Charge – up to 4 times (13.3%), 5 to 10 (5%), 11 to 15 (1.7%), 16 and above (1.7%), no meetings (58.3%), many times (20%). Meeting with MP – up to 4 times (8.3%), 5 to 10 (3.4%), no meetings (88.3%), many times (5%). Meeting with Chief Minister – up to 4 times (5%), no meetings (95%).

Table 5.37

Have you Contacted the Following?

Individual	*Up to 4 times*	*5 to 10*	*11 to 15*	*16 and above*	*No Meeting*	*Many times*
Janpad CEO	10 (16.7)	4 (06.7)	01 (01.7)	-	30 (50.0)	15 (25.0)
Janpad Chairperson	09 (15.0)	2 (03.4)	01 (01.7)	01 (01.7)	29 (48.3)	18 (30.0)
Zilla Panchayat CEO	09 (15.0)	03 (05.1)	-	-	41 (68.3)	07(11.7)
Zilla Panchayat Chairperson	05 (08.3)	02 (03.4)	-	01 (01.7)	42 (70.0)	10 (16.7)
Collector	05 (08.3)	-	-	-	53 (88.3)	02 (03.3)
MLA	08 (13.3)	06 (10.0)	01 (01.7)	01 (01.7)	26 (43.3)	18 (30.0)
Minister-in-charge	08 (13.3)	03 (05.0)	01 (01.7)	01 (01.7)	35 (58.3)	12 (20.0)
MP	05 (08.3)	02 (03.4)	-	-	50 (83.3)	03 (05.0)
Chief Minister	03 (05.0)	-	-	-	57 (95.0)	-

Figures in parentheses are percentages.

Thus, it is clear from the above analysis that in majority cases there was no meeting with important individuals who could have helped in the solution of the problem/s. It is obvious because in the sample Up-sarpanch and Panch are also included whereas usually the meetings with important individuals is done by Sarpanch. The figures show that large number of respondents have contacted all important individuals/officers, etc., time and again. It clearly confirms that the local leadership has developed the practice of contacting all the important individuals/officers for panchayat work.

After knowing this fact, it has been traced out as what were the reasons to meet these individuals. The reasons are given as under:

Reasons for meeting Janpad CEO: for school problem (3), related to Gram Sabha (15), related to welfare schemes (2), for government work (3), for stop dam (2), general meeting (1), for training (1).

Reasons for meeting Janpad Chairperson: for village problem (17), related to Gram Sabha (5), related to welfare schemes (2), for panchayat work (2), for stop dam (1), general meeting (2), for grants (1).

Reasons for meeting Zilla Panchayat CEO: for village problem (13), related to welfare schemes (5).

Reasons for meeting Zilla Panchayat Chairperson: for village problem (9), related to welfare schemes (2), for grants (1), for construction work (2), for development work (2).

Reasons for meeting Collector: for village problem (3), for personal work (2).

Reasons for meeting MLA: for village problem (17), for development work (3), for school (1), personal work (2), for construction of building (1) for MLA fund (8), for demand letter (1).

Reasons for meeting Minister-in-Charge: for village problem (12), for development work (4), for personal work (4), for MLA fund (4).

Reasons for meeting MP: for village problem (6), for community building (1), for personal work (1), for MP fund (1).

Reasons for meeting Chief Minister – for grants (2).

The reasons mentioned for the meetings clearly underline that the meetings were arranged for seeking help in village development programmes, for better execution of welfare programmes or for extra funds needed for panchayat activities.

Dominance in Panchayat/Gram Sabha

Table 5.38 provides the details regarding the question as who dominates Panchayat/Gram Sabha. Around 65 per cent respondents are of the view that nobody dominates the Panchayat/Gram Sabha. Nearly 15 per cent respondents point out that Sarpanch dominates the Panchayat/Gram Sabha. Only 10 per cent respondents express the view that Panchayat/Gram Sabha is dominated by anti social elements and. 5 per cent respondents say that educated people dominate Panchayat/Gram Sabha. One respondent each, points out that Panchayat/Gram Sabha is dominated by socio-economic elites and higher caste people, whereas remaining one respondent does not know about this problem.

Table 5.38

Dominance in Panchayat/Gram Sabha

Dominant Group	*Number of Respondents*	*Percentage*
Sarpanch	09	15.0
Socio-economic elite	01	01.7
Higher caste people	01	01.7
Educated people	03	05.0
Anti-social elements	06	10.0
Don't know	01	01.7
Nobody	39	65.0
Total	60	100.0

The above analysis clearly depicts that almost two-thirds respondents feel that nobody dominates Panchayat/Gram Sabha. It is indeed a positive and encouraging sign that respondents do not have the feeling that there is any domination either of a person or of any outside agency. Of course, Sarpanch and anti-social elements have been referred as dominant groups that should be a real cause for worry for the Panchayat/Gram Sabha.

Contentious Issues in Panchayat/Gram Sabha

Table 5.39 describes the issues that are contentious in nature that harm homogeneity of Panchayat/Gram Sabha. As much as 86.7 per cent respondents are of the view that no such issue exists here which becomes a bone of contention for Panchayat/Gram Sabha members. Casteism is as an issue of that nature in the opinion of 3.3 per cent respondents with another 3.3 per cent respondents feeling that selection of beneficiaries is the cause. One respondent argues that election for any post becomes the cause of contention. Remaining two respondents do not know the reason of such contentious issues.

Table 5.39

Bone of Contentions in Panchayat/Gram Sabha

Reason	*Number of Respondents*	*Percentage*
Casteism	02	03.3
Formation and implementation of schemes	01	01.7
Election on a post	01	01.7
Selection of beneficiaries	02	03.3
Never	52	86.7
Don't know	02	03.3
Total	60	100.0

Thus, it is clear from the above analysis that an overwhelming majority of the respondents point out that they never find any issue which becomes a bone of contention among Panchayat/Gram Sabha members. It is definitely a matter of big satisfaction that Panchayat/Gram Sabha are not made platforms where disputable questions are raised and discussed.

Table 5.40

Representation of Different Groups in Panchayat for Better Performance

Group	*Yes*	*No*	*Not Necessary*	*Total*
Higher caste	05 (08.3)	08 (13.3)	47 (78.3)	60 (100.0)
Educated people	51 (85.0)	02 (03.3)	07 (11.7)	60 (100.0)
Rich people	03 (05.0)	10 (16.7)	47 (78.3)	60 (100.0)
Male as compared to female	12 (20.0)	06 (10.0)	42 (70.0)	60 (100.0)
Politically active	23 (38.3)	09 (15.0)	28 (46.7)	60 (100.0)
Religious person	20 (33.3)	08 (13.3)	32 (53.3)	60 (100.0)
Government employee	18 (30.0)	07 (11.7)	35 (58.3)	60 (100.0)
People having village development attitude	54 (90.0)	01 (01.7)	05 (08.3)	60 (100.0)
Local leader	47 (78.3)	04 (06.7)	09 (15.0)	60 (100.0)

Figures in parentheses are percentages.

Opinion was sought about the representation of different groups in panchayat for better performance. Table 5.40 presents views regarding this question. Opinion regarding higher caste for better performance – yes (8.3%), no (13.3%), not necessary (78.3%). Opinion regarding educated people for better performance – yes (85%), no (3.3%), not necessary (11.7%). Opinion regarding rich people for better performance – yes (5%), no (16.7%), not necessary (78.3%). Opinion regarding male as compared to female for better performance – yes (20%), no (10%), not necessary (70%). Opinion regarding politically active people for better performance – yes (38.3%), no (15%), not necessary (46.7%). Opinion regarding religious persons for better performance – yes (33.3%), no (13.3%), not necessary (53.3%). Opinion regarding government employee for better performance – yes (30%), no (11.7%), not necessary (58.3%). Opinion regarding people having village development orientations for better performance – yes (90%), no (1.7%), not necessary (8.3%). Opinion regarding local leader for better performance – yes (78.3%), no (6.7%), not necessary (15%).

The above analysis clearly depicts that people having village development orientations, educated people and local leaders are considered good for better performance of panchayats. This demonstrates that at local level conceptually the respondents agree to have better leadership.

Inspection Done by Panchayat

Panchayats are empowered to perform as units of self-governance. Government of Madhya Pradesh has delegated several powers and authorised panchayat representatives to inspect government offices to see for themselves whether the departments were working properly. Looking into this aspect an effort was made to know respondents' viewpoint regarding inspection.

Table 5.41

Have you Inspected any of the Following Places as a Panchayat Representative?

Places	*Yes*	*No*	*Total*
School	43 (71.7)	17 (28.3)	60 (100.0)
Anganwadi	38 (63.3)	22 (36.7)	60 (100.0)
Water supply	24 (40.0)	36 (60.0)	60 (100.0)
Streetlight	18 (30.0)	42 (70.0)	60 (100.0)
Health centre	24 (40.0)	36 (60.0)	60 (100.0)
Welfare schemes	41 (68.3)	19 (31.7)	60 (100.0)
Construction work	40 (66.7)	20 (33.3)	60 (100.0)
Development work	40 (66.7)	20 (33.3)	60 (100.0)

Figures in parentheses are percentages.

Table 5.41 describes the details of the inspection of public welfare departments and municipal services by the panchayat representatives. The place-wise details are as follows: inspection of school is done by 71.7 per cent respondents; inspection of 'Anganwadi' is done by 63.3 per cent respondents; inspection of water supply is done by 40 per cent; inspection of street lights is done by 30 per cent; inspection of health centre is done by 40 per cent; inspection of welfare schemes is done by 68.3 per cent; inspection of construction work is done by 66.7 per cent respondents and inspection of development works is done by 66.7 per cent respondents.

Such details give a fair picture of deep involvement of panchayat representatives in local affairs. It is a positive indication that in majority cases school, 'Anganwadi', welfare schemes, construction work and development works are inspected from time to time by people's representatives. In fact, these are important public departments and service-providing agencies at grassroots level. Since streetlights and water supply are not provided by panchayats in many cases, panchayat representatives do not have any role in supervising/inspecting such activities.

Gram Kosh

Historically speaking, the Gram Kosh is a very old time-effective system at the village level. After a passage of time this institution was out of practice in villages. Looking into the rich legacy and vibrancy of such system it has been revived under Gram Swaraj.

Table 5.42

Whether Gram Kosh is Established in Your Village?

Gram Kosh Established	*Number of Respondents*	*Percentage*
Yes	27	45.0
No	33	55.0
Total	60	100.0

Table 5.42 explains the establishment of Gram Kosh in villages. Nearly 45 per cent respondents say that Gram Kosh has been established in their villages under the new system whereas 55 per cent respondents say 'No'. It is thus clear that one very important aspect of Gram Swaraj is at least known to almost half of the respondents.

The Gram Kosh includes four components – Anna Kosh, Shram Kosh, Vastu Kosh and Nagad Kosh. Anna Kosh is known to 26.7 per cent respondents. Shram Kosh is known to 20 per cent respondents and 15 per cent respondents know about the Vastu Kosh. Nagad Kosh is known to 35 per cent respondents. These

Koshas have been under the Gram Swaraj to help villagers in their difficult days. It is indeed surprising that majority of the panchayat representatives are ignorant about these Koshas.

Table 5.43

Do you Know the Following Koshas?

Kosh	*Know*	*Don't Know*	*Total*
Anna (Grain)	16 (26.7)	44 (73.3)	60 (100.0)
Shram (Labour)	12 (20.0)	48 (80.0)	60 (100.0)
Vastu (Articles)	09 (15.0)	51 (85.0)	60 (100.0)
Nagad (Cash)	21 (35.0)	39 (65.0)	60 (100.0)

Figures in parentheses are percentages.

Koshadhyaksha (Treasurer) in Gram Swaraj

The office of Koshadhyaksha (Treasurer) has been a controversial one in the working of Gram Swaraj. It has been argued by Sarpanch and his coterie that the creation of the post of Koshadhyaksha is to undermine the position of Sarpanch. The funds available at the Gram Panchayat level are very limited and all these funds are to be utilised with the consent of Gram Sabha but the post of Koshadhyaksha has remained the bone of contention at occasions.

Table 5.44

Election of Koshadhyaksha

Basis of Election	*Number of Respondents*	*Percentage*
Unanimously	47	78.3
On the basis of caste	03	05.0
As desired by local leaders	04	06.7
Through Gram Sabha	02	03.3
Through election	01	01.7
Don't know	03	05.0
Total	60	100.0

Table 5.44 throws light on the election procedure of Koshadhyaksha. Whereas 78.3 per cent respondents are of the view that the election was unanimous, 6.7 per cent respondents point out that it was as desired by local leaders. Around 5 per cent respondents present the fact that it was on the basis of caste with 3.3 per cent respondents arguing that it was through Gram Sabha and 1.7 per cent respondents are of the view that it was through election. Remaining 5 per cent respondents do not know the procedure. This shows that majority of respondents favour the unanimous elections.

Work Done by the Last Panchayat

Empowerment of panchayat is basically to have maximum participation of people in the decision-making and in all other important activities. The concept of social audit is also very important from the point of view of awareness of panchayat representatives towards the work done by panchayat.

Table 5.45

Do you have the Following Information Related to Last Work done by your Panchayat?

Panchayat Work	*Yes*	*No*	*Total*
Work name	36 (60.0)	24 (40.0)	60 (100.0)
Cost of the work	26 (43.3)	34 (56.7)	60 (100.0)
Allotment received	26 (43.3)	34 (56.7)	60 (100.0)
Total expenditure	26 (43.3)	34 (56.7)	60 (100.0)
Completion period	33 (55.0)	27 (56.7)	60 (100.0)
Availability and quality of material	34 (56.7)	26 (43.3)	60 (100.0)
Construction agency/contractor	34 (56.7)	26 (43.3)	60 (100.0)

Figures in parentheses are percentages.

Table 5.45 describes the understanding of panchayat representatives for the last work done by the panchayat. As much as 60 per cent respondents know the name of the last work done by the panchayat, 43.3 per cent respondents know the cost of the work, and 43.3 per cent respondents know the allotment received. Also 43.3 per cent respondents know the total expenditure incurred on the work, 55 per cent respondents know the period of completion of work, 56.7 per cent respondents know the availability and quality of construction material used and 56.7 per cent respondents know the construction agency. It explains that a large number of respondents is well versed with all the steps for the completion of a work along with the details of each activity. This awareness is good for panchayat working.

Committee System in Gram Swaraj

The most important innovation introduced through Gram Swaraj is the committee system. The basic idea behind having different committees is to ascertain the participation of different groups, particularly the stakeholders. Assigning work to different committees brings in efficiency and location of responsibility in panchayat working. It is also a make of division of labour and ensuring work input from panchayat members.

Table 5.46

Membership of the Committees under Gram Swaraj

Membership	*Number of Respondents*	*Percentage*
Village Development Committee	06	10.0
Village Security Committee	04	06.7
Agriculture Committee	02	03.3
Education Committee	06	10.0
Health Committee	03	05.0
Infrastructure Committee	02	03.3
Social Justice Committee	03	05.0
No membership	34	56.7
Total	60	100.0

Table 5.46 describes the membership of particular committees to which the respondents belong. Village Development Committee (6), Village Security Committee (4), Agriculture Committee (2),

Education Committee (6), Health Committee (3), Infrastructure Committee (2), and Social Justice Committee (3). Remaining 34 respondents are not members of any committee.

It clearly provides a fair picture that the selected respondents represent various committees but they are small in number whereas majority of the respondents are not members of any committee.

The basic idea behind having different committees is to have a decentralised pattern of decision-making. It provides ample opportunity to villagers, particularly the representatives of marginalised sections of the society and stakeholders to take part in committee meetings and raise their voice about the issues of larger interest for all.

Table 5.47

Committee Meetings Held

Meeting Held	*Number of Respondents*	*Percentage*
Yes	26	43.3
No	34	56.7
Total	60	100.0

Table 5.47 describes the details whether committee meetings are held. Around 43.3 per cent respondents are of the view that meetings are held whereas remaining 56.7 per cent respondents point out that the meetings are not held. It suggests that less than half of the respondents are of the opinion that meetings are held. It is definitely a democratic and systematic way of functioning of panchayats. However, people are not fully aware about the committee system and its importance. This is the reason that the committee meetings are not held regularly.

Table 5.48 shows the issues raised or discussed in meetings. In all, 26 respondents are of the view that meetings are held about the issues related to matters of village life. According to seven respondents, the question of education was raised; two respondents mentioned about health and ten respondents about development issues. According to two respondents, issues related to agriculture were raised. However, two of them are critical that there was no discussion at all about such issues.

Table 5.48
If Yes, Issues in Meeting

Issues	*Number of Respondents*	*Percentage*
Related to education	07	11.7
Health related	02	03.3
Development related	10	16.7
Related to water	01	01.7
Agriculture related	02	03.3
No discussion	02	03.3
Don't know	02	03.3
Total	26	43.3

Thus, it is very clear from the responses that all major issues related to village are discussed in committee meetings.

Opinion about Gram Swaraj

Table 5.49 describes opinions of respondents about the nature, utility and significance of Gram Swaraj. Whereas 55 per cent respondents are of the view that it is a good system, 5 per cent respondents feel that power has now been transferred to villagers through this system. Around 3.3 per cent respondents are of the view that Sarpanch's powers are transferred to Gram Sabha and panchayat's works have become public with five per cent respondents pointing out that all works are done/all village-related problems are solved in village itself by the village people. On the contrary, 3.3 per cent respondents feel that panchayat has become an arena for people to fight while 10 per cent respondents feel that all members do not get equal treatment in meetings, whereas remaining 15 per cent respondents have nothing to say about the new system.

Table 5.49

Opinion about Gram Swaraj

Opinion	*Number of Respondents*	*Percentage*
Good system	33	55.0
Power transferred to villagers	03	05.0
Sarpanch's powers are transferred to Gram Sabha	02	03.3
Panchayat's work has become public	02	03.3
All works are done/all village problems are solved now	03	05.0
People fight	02	03.3
All are not getting due weightage	06	10.0
Don't know	09	15.0
Total	60	100.0

It is thus clear from the above analysis that opinions about Gram Swaraj is of a mixed nature but its positive aspects are more than the negative ones; that has a significant meaning for the system of Gram Swaraj.

Changes Discernible in Caste Differentiation due to Gram Swaraj

Table 5.50 explains the changes discernible in the caste differentiation due to Gram Swaraj. Around 40 per cent respondents find that untouchability and partiality have decreased; 13.3 per cent respondents feel that all sit in the meetings as equals; 3.3 per cent respondents are of the view that now everything is decided unanimously; 6.7 per cent respondents point out that caste differentiations have decreased and 1 respondent argues that the marginalised section of society have become aware of rights. On the contrary 20 per cent respondents are of the view that there is no change in social order whereas 10 per cent respondents point out that casteism has increased. Remaining 5 per cent respondents merely say 'don't know'.

Table 5.50

Is There any Change Discernible in the Caste Differentiation due to Gram Swaraj?

Change	*Number of Respondents*	*Percentage*
Untouchability and partiality decreased	24	40.0
Equal respect to all	08	13.3
Now every thing is decided unanimously	02	03.3
Caste disabilities decreased	04	06.7
Marginalised section is becoming aware	01	01.7
No difference	12	20.0
Casteism increased	06	10.0
Don't know	03	05.0
Total	60	100.0

Thus, it is clear from the above analysis that due to Gram Swaraj caste differentiations has decreased; this is the view of majority respondents.

Selection of Beneficiaries

Table 5.51 interprets the changes discernible in the selection of beneficiaries due to Gram Swaraj. With 25 per cent respondents of the view that the selection is done unanimously, 15 per cent respondents feel that now the selection is done appropriately and judiciously; five per cent respondents point out that positive change has come in the selection process; one respondent is of the view that now decisions are taken in village only; 8.3 per cent respondents argue that still it is according to the sweet will of the Sarpanch; 23.4 per cent respondents find that there is no change; and one respondent is of the view that as no meeting takes place and the whole question is irrelevant. Remaining 18.3 per cent respondents donot know about this.

Table 5.51

Is There any Change Discernible in the Selection of Beneficiaries due to Gram Swaraj?

Change	*Number of Respondents*	*Percentage*
Selection is done unanimously	15	25.0
Appropriate selection	09	15.0
Positive change has come	03	05.0
According to Sarpanch	05	08.3
Now, the decisions are taken in village only	01	01.7
No change	14	23.4
Now it is disputed	01	01.7
No meeting takes place	01	01.7
Don't know	11	18.3
Total	60	100.0

There were times when fingers were raised about the selection procedure of beneficiaries. However, with the introduction of Gram Swaraj, fairness has entered in the selection process.

Change in the Behaviour of Socio-economic Elites

Village society is different from the urban one which retains strong feudal characteristics even after more than 5 decades of independence. Such socio-economic elites have been playing vital and judgmental roles in the villages.

Table 5.52 observes the changes discernible in the behaviour and attitudes of socio-economic elites due to Gram Swaraj. With 71.7 per cent respondents of the view that there is no change in this respect, 5 per cent respondents point out that their mindset has changed; 18.4 per cent respondents opine that there is a gradual change in their attitudes whereas remaining 5 per cent respondents can not say anything about it.

Table 5.52

Is There any Change Discernible in the Behaviour of Socio-economic Elites due to Gram Swaraj?

Change	*Number of Respondents*	*Percentage*
No change	43	71.7
Mindset has changed	03	05.0
Gradual change in the attitude	11	18.4
Can't say	03	05.0
Total	60	100.0

Thus, it is clear from the above analysis that overwhelming majority of the respondents feel no change in the attitude of socio-economic elites. It is indeed a matter of concern from the point of view of village society and smooth functioning of Gram Sabha. It is therefore urgently needed to sensitise the elites as well as village society about the values of equality for the sake of establishing a new social order.

Changes Needed in Gram Swaraj

Table 5.53 analyses the changes needed for Gram Swaraj. Only 6.7 per cent respondents feel that committees should get more power and 11.7 per cent respondents find that all the decisions should be taken at panchayat; 3.3 per cent respondents are of the view that senior persons should be included in committees; 1.7 per cent respondents point out that all the committees should get separate grants; five per cent respondents argue that one person should be made wholesole; 1.7 per cent respondents feel that the post of koshadhyaksha should be abolished; 6.7 per cent respondents are of the view that the Gram Sabha should not be made dependent on Janpad or Zilla Panchayat; and 35 per cent respondents point out that no change is needed in the existing system.

Replies given by a small number of respondents suggest that only few changes are needed here and there in the Act whereas a sizeable numbers advocate no change. Such replies fortify the credibility of the new system.

Table 5.53

What Kind of Change is Needed in Gram Swaraj System?

Change Needed	*Number of Respondents*	*Percentage*
Committees should get more power	04	06.7
All works should be done at panchayat	07	11.7
Senior persons should be included in committees	02	03.3
All committees should get separate grants	01	01.7
One person should be made wholesole	03	05.0
The post of Koshadhyaksha should be abolished	01	01.7
Gram Sabha should not be made dependent on Janpad Panchayat or Zilla Panchayat	04	06.7
No change is needed	21	35.0
Don't know	17	28.3
Total	60	100.0

Changes at Local Level due to Gram Swaraj

Table 5.54 describes the changes discernible at local level due to Gram Swaraj. Around 55 per cent respondents find that development works have been carried out in villages; one respondent feels that people have been benefited by schemes and all panchayat

Table 5.54

Is There any Change Discernible at Local Level due to Gram Swaraj?

Change	*Number of Respondents*	*Percentage*
Development work carried out in villages	33	55.0
People get benefit of schemes	01	01.7
All works are transparent	01	01.7
No change	12	20.0
Less development	06	10.0
No development	01	01.7
Don't know	06	10.0
Total	60	100.0

works are transparent; 20 per cent respondents are of the view that no change has been brought about by Gram Swaraj; 10 per cent respondents point out that there is little development; one respondent argues that there is no development at all whereas 10 per cent respondents do not have any idea about these matters.

Thus, it is clear from the above analysis that more than half of the respondents feel that development works are done whereas one-fifth respondents do not find any change at local level because of Gram Swaraj.

Problems and Weaknesses of Gram Swaraj

Table 5.55 illustrates the problems and weaknesses in the functioning of Gram Swaraj. Nearly 16.7 per cent respondents feel that people do not know about Gram Swaraj; 3.3 per cent respondents equally point out that there is non-supportive attitude of local elites and quorum is always a problem; 5 per cent respondents are of the view that Koshadhyaksha is not supportive; one respondent complains that groupism has increased in the villages; 6.7 per cent respondents feel that work is not done timely; 28.3 per cent respondents do not know any problem whereas 33.3 per cent respondents do not find any problem with the working of the system.

Table 5.55

Problems and Weaknesses of Gram Swaraj

Problems and Weaknesses	*Number of Respondents*	*Percentage*
People don't know about Gram Swaraj	10	16.7
Non supportive attitude of local elite	02	03.3
Quorum is not possible	02	03.3
Koshadhyaksha is not supportive	03	05.0
Groupism increased	01	01.7
Work is not done timely	04	06.7
No problem	17	28.3
Don't know	20	33.3

In fact, due to lack of exposure and understanding of the Gram Swaraj the number of persons acquainted with the problems are very limited and also a considerable number of them do not know about any problem in the working of Gram Swaraj.

Suggestions to Improve the Gram Swaraj System

Table 5.56 provides suggestions to improve the Gram Swaraj system. About 23.3 per cent respondents are of the view that finance related problems should be solved because in the last analysis that money makes the mare go is true of the panchayat system also; 3.3 per cent respondents equally point out that Sarpanch should take initiatives to bring all villagers together and committees should be represented by eligible persons, and not through reservations; 8.3 per cent respondents feel that committees should be made powerful and more specific; five per cent respondents argue that all the schemes should be evaluated locally; 8.3 per cent respondents suggest that people should be informed more about Gram Swaraj; one respondent equally is of the view that the interference of government officials should be minimised and the post of koshadhyaksha should be abolished; and 51.7 per cent respondents do not have any suggestions to make.

Table 5.56

Suggestions to Improve Gram Swaraj

Suggestions	*Number of Respondents*	*Percentage*
Finance related problems should be solved	15	23.3
Sarpanch should take initiatives to bring all villagers together	02	03.3
No reservation/committees should be represented by eligible persons	02	03.3
Committees should be made powerful and more specific	05	08.3
All the schemes should be evaluated locally	03	05.0
People should be more informed about Gram Swaraj	05	08.3
The interference of govt. officials should be eliminated	01	01.7
The post of Koshadhyaksha should be abolished	01	01.7
No suggestions	31	51.7

Thus, it is clear from the above analysis that almost half of the respondents have suggestions to improve the Gram Swaraj system, which is very significant in many respects. Awareness generation and educating people have come out as significant suggestions whereas some other important suggestions have also been made to improve Gram Swaraj system.

To conclude, it can be inferred that all the categories in the selected village population are properly represented in the sample. The majority group of respondents is below the age of 50. The representation of male and female is in four-one ratio. Majority of respondents are educated up to various levels. Educational level of respondents is considerably very good. Majority of the respondents do agriculture work and a significant number of respondents are housewives.

Three-fourths of respondents are of the view that their candidature for panchayat was decided by villagers. It is indeed a positive indication for democracy at local level. It is also a matter of satisfaction that by election, two-thirds respondents have come in panchayat whereas one-third entered in panchayat unopposed. In majority cases the respondents do not have any previous experience of the working in panchayat.

It is interesting to note that overwhelming majority of the respondents feel that meetings are regular. The respondents have pointed out some specific reasons for non-regularity of panchayat meetings. It is a positive indication that almost three-fourths of the respondents attend the meetings regularly. Respondents have pointed out lack of timely information and personal work as the major reasons for not attending the meetings of panchayat. Majority of the respondents discuss issues in panchayat meetings. Almost one-fourth respondents play an idle role, nevertheless the positive majority opinion matters with respect to functioning.

Half of the respondents visit Tehsil and Janpad Panchayat. A considerable number of them visit Zilla Panchayat. Remaining offices are visited by a limited number. The exposure of respondents clearly demonstrates that the Sarpanch, secretary and some other representatives visit the offices for panchayat work. The visits are mostly done for the sake of solving village problem, panchayat work or official work. Though the number is limited but it is important that they are well versed with the functional and operational aspect of panchayat.

MLA is the most known person to the respondents. Chairperson of Zilla and Janpad Panchayat and Minister-in-Charge is also known by a significant number of respondents. Since these persons are directly involved in helping panchayats for various works, the local leadership is more exposed about them. Collector, once the most powerful district official, is the least known name to local leadership now.

It is indeed a matter of concern that almost half of respondents have made efforts for doing some work in panchayat and that too when among the respondents very few are Sarpanch and remaining are Panch. It is a very encouraging and positive sign that in majority opinion the selection of beneficiaries is done as per the rules. Though one-fourth respondents still feel that Sarpanch/secretary fulfil this job.

It is indeed a matter of big satisfaction that overwhelming majority point out regularity of Gram Sabha meetings, which is of very significance from the point of view of success of Gram Swaraj system in Madhya Pradesh. It is interesting to note that almost two-thirds of the respondents know this factual information. Overwhelming percentage is well aware of the women's presence required for quorum of Gram Sabha meetings. It is a positive indication that this significant aspect of mandatory women participation is known by a considerable number. A significant percentage of respondents are regularly participating in the meetings. Only a very small number never participated in the meetings. Major reasons shown by the respondents for not attending the meetings are their extraordinary busy schedule, not getting information and nobody listens.

Training has not been adequately carried out to make the panchayat representatives aware about the procedural aspect of Gram Swaraj. The respondents have mainly received the training from district or block headquarters. The respondents have mainly received basic clarity about Gram Swaraj through training.

Local problem is the main issue of discussion in meetings. Almost three-fourths respondents have expressed their views that the decisions are unanimous. It confirms that slowly and gradually people are getting closer to the issues of panchayats. It is a positive indication that three-fourths respondents are contacted by the villagers for panchayat related work. The respondents have pointed out reason of meeting villagers are village problem or personal problem.

In most of the cases either the problems are decreased after formation of Gram Swaraj or has remained same. Exceptionally the health problem is referred as increased. After discussing all the solutions for different problems before and after Gram Swaraj, it is clear that the solution procedure remained more or less same. It can be so because, first, the new system has spent a very little span of time and second, the issues are of the nature that they cannot be solved within the given situation and resources.

In majority cases there is no meeting with important individuals. It is obvious because in sample we have selected Up-sarpanch and Panch as well and usually the meetings with important individuals is done by Sarpanch. Even than a considerable number have contacted all important individuals many times. It clearly confirms that the local leadership is contacting all the important individuals for panchayat work.

Almost two-thirds respondents feel that nobody dominated Panchayat/Gram Sabha. It is indeed a positive and encouraging sign that usually respondents do not observe that there is any domination. Though Sarpanch and anti-social elements are also referred as dominant groups that is a real cause for worry for the Panchayat/Gram Sabha.

Overwhelming majority of the respondents make their point that they never find any issue as a bone of contention in Panchayat/Gram Sabha. It is definitely a matter of big satisfaction that Panchayat/Gram Sabha are not the platforms where disputes are raised and discussed.

People having village development attitude, educated people and local leaders are considered good for better performance in panchayat. It demonstrates that at local level conceptually the respondents agree to have better leadership.

It is a positive indication that in majority cases school, anganwadi, welfare schemes, construction work and development work are inspected. Usually, these are prominent works at grass-roots level. Since streetlight and water supply are not provided by panchayats in many cases and therefore they do not have any role to inspect such activities.

Almost half of the respondents know the Gram Kosh and out of them a considerable number know the various koshas under Gram Kosh. Majority respondents' opinion is in favour of unanimous election of Koshadhyaksha. A considerable number is well versed with all the steps for the completion of a work along with the details of each activity. This awareness is a good depiction of healthy scenario for the better and transparent functioning of panchayats.

The selected respondents represent various committees but in small number, whereas majority respondents are not members of any committee. Less than half of the respondents point out that meeting is held. It is definitely a new innovation and through committees specific issues are to be discussed but people are not made properly aware about the committee system and therefore the committee meetings are not happening in majority cases. In committee meetings, all major issues related to village are discussed in committee meetings.

The opinion about Gram Swaraj is of mix nature but the positive opinion is outweighting the negative that has a significant meaning for the system of Gram Swaraj. Due to Gram Swaraj caste differentiation is decreased from the point of view of majority respondents. Though there are views that there is no difference or casteism increased but nevertheless in majority opinion, caste differentiation is decreased due to Gram Swaraj.

Significant number of respondents believe that the due procedure is adopted whereas almost one-fourth of the respondents do not find any change. Since the fingers have been raised on the selection procedure of beneficiaries prior to Gram Swaraj it is indeed a positive feedback that in majority opinion the selection is adhered with due procedure.

Only few changes are suggested by a small number of respondents, whereas a sizeable number advocate for no change. It promotes the credibility of the new system. Overwhelming majority of the respondents feel no change in the attitude of socio-economic elite. It is indeed a matter of concern from the point of view of village society and smooth functioning of Gram Sabha; it is urgently needed to sensitise the village society for the socio-economic equity and awareness for equal opportunities of occasions for everyone.

In fact, due to lack of exposure and understanding of the Gram Swaraj the number of persons acquainted with the problem are very limited and also a considerable number either do not know any problem or do not find any problem nevertheless all the possible problems are cited by respondents.

Almost half of the respondents have suggestions to improve the Gram Swaraj system, which is very significant in many respects. Awareness generation and educating people have come out as significant suggestions, whereas other important suggestions have also come out.

6

Gram Sabha Members' Participation, Attitudes and Perceptions Towards Gram Swaraj: An Analysis

Gram Swaraj has emerged from an extensive process of deliberations, refinements and dialogue. It is also a result of the grassroots experiences of functioning of Panchayat Raj, coupled with Madhya Pradesh government's stated commitment to democratic decentralisation. The Gandhian ideological framework provided the basic structure and body to this new system of self-governance. The primary objective of introducing a new system of Gram Swaraj is evidently to transfer power to the people and to sincerely take forward the process of democratic decentralisation to its logical end. The new structure is substantially influenced by Gandhian commitment to Gram Swaraj to facilitate social, economic and political autonomy at the village level. It needs to be appreciated that Gram Swaraj is an attempt to radically restructure the governance space according to Gandhian worldview. Gram Swaraj is also an attempt to reduce groupism and animosity being created due to panchayat elections. According to the votaries of Gram Swaraj, experience suggests that loss in elections is taken as a personal loss in a village, often leading to disruption of the social fabric. With the strengthening of Gram Sabha and introduction of Gram Swaraj, gradually the panchayat elections would not be hotly contested and the disruption of the society would be stalled.

Gram Swaraj system is to organise separate Gram Sabhas for each village. In Madhya Pradesh a Gram Panchayat is often constituted of more than one village. To do justice to each village and to make the system of Gram Swaraj effective it was imperative to recognise the Gram Sabha of each village as independent. However, to resolve issues affecting the whole Gram Panchayat a provision of joint Gram Sabha has also been inserted. Another important objective of Gram Swaraj is to reassert village as a social unit. The attempt has been made to help resurrect the village community, which was disintegrating causing considerable adverse consequences.

Against this backdrop, the study is designed to investigate the functioning of Gram Swaraj as well as to fully understand the attitudes and perceptions of the Gram Sabha members. A structured interview schedule was administered for this purpose. Besides this, informal discussions and field observations were also of help to provide inputs to strengthen data analysis and the arguments involved. This chapter analyses in detail the various facets of Gram Swaraj from the point of view of Gram Sabha members.

Caste

After 73rd Amendment Act, due representation has been given to all the castes to participate in the panchayat affairs. Through Gram Swaraj, it has been ascertained that particularly the weaker and marginalised sections of the society are duly represented in the decision-making process of the Gram Sabha.

Keeping in view the provisions of the new Act, the Gram Sabha members were chosen from different castes and communities for the study. Table 6.1 shows that 52.5 per cent respondents are from the OBC category and 32.5 per cent represent the general group. Remaining 15 per cent respondents are from the SC category. Thus, it is clear from the above analysis that all the three categories in the selected village population are properly represented in the sample.

Table 6.1
Caste

Caste	*Number of Respondents*	*Percentage*
General	39	32.5
Scheduled Castes	18	15.0
OBCs	63	52.5
Total	120	100.0

Age

An effort has been made in this section to know about the age of the selected respondents as age is one of important aspects concerned with the present study. It shows the background of experience of the respondents that come with age. For purposes of analysis, age has been categorised in four groups as 18 to 25, 26 to 40, 41 to 55 and 56 and above.

Table 6.2
Age

Age Group	*Number of Respondents*	*Percentage*
18 to 25	13	10.8
26 to 40	60	50.0
41 to 55	26	21.7
56 and above	21	17.5
Total	120	100.0

Table 6.2 reveals that 50 per cent respondents fall in the age group of 26 to 40 and 21.7 per cent respondents are from the age

group of 41 to 55, 17.5 per cent respondents belong to the age group of 56 and above, whereas rest 10.8 per cent respondents represent age group of 18 to 25. It clearly demonstrates that the majority of the respondents is below the age of 40.

Sex

Sex is a very important indicator in analysing socio-economic characteristics of the respondents. It is also assumed that the level of exposure, awareness and points of views of both the sexes are different particularly in rural scenario. Thus the factor of sex has been kept in view while constructing the sample. The following table is an indicator of sex variable of the respondents:

Table 6.3
Sex

Sex	*Number of Respondents*	*Percentage*
Male	82	68.3
Female	38	31.7
Total	120	100.0

Table 6.3 indicates that 68.3 per cent respondents are male whereas the representation of female is 31.7 per cent. Since one-third representation of females has been made mandatory for the quorum of Gram Sabha meeting, it substantiates the fact that the sample is also represented by almost one-third female respondents.

Education

Education is also one of the basic indices to assess the socio-economic status of an individual. Since Independence, efforts have been made to provide educational facilities to all sections of society. A certain minimum level of literacy is the basic requirement for the people to get out of the trap of ignorance and backwardness. Despite all efforts to enhance the levels of literacy, the scenario is still disappointing in the rural area particularly for the marginalised sections and for women.

Table 6.4
Education

Education	*Number of Respondents*	*Percentage*
Illiterate	32	26.7
Literate	06	05.0
Primary	35	29.2
Secondary	27	22.5
Higher Secondary	16	13.3
Graduate and above	04	03.3
Total	120	100.0

Table 6.4 reflects that 29.2 per cent respondents are educated up to primary, 22.5 per cent respondents are educated up to secondary level and only 13.3 per cent respondents are educated up to higher secondary level. Only 3.3 per cent respondents are educated up to graduate and above. Remaining 26.7 per cent respondents are illiterate. Thus, it is clear from the analysis that almost three-fourths of the respondents are educated up to various levels. Looking into the rural background of respondents wherein one-third are female, it appears that the educational level is considerably very good.

Occupation

Occupation is also one of the very important indices to analyse the background of the respondents. In rural India occupation of the majority of the population is either agriculture or labour.

Table 6.5 shows that 55 per cent respondents are engaged in agriculture work, 25.8 per cent respondents are housewives and 8.3 per cent respondents equally are engaged in labour and business work. Remaining 2.5 per cent respondents are in service. Thus, it clearly shows that majority of the respondents do agriculture work.

Table 6.5
Occupation

Occupation	*Number of Respondents*	*Percentage*
Agriculture	66	55.0
Labour	10	08.3
Business	10	08.3
Service	03	02.5
Housewife	31	25.8
Total	120	100.0

Gram Sabha

The legislative empowerment of the Gram Sabha in India is a political development of utmost importance because it marks the clearest break from the most dominant political orthodoxy of this century so far as rural India is concerned. In Madhya Pradesh special efforts have been made to empower the Gram Sabha.

Table 6.6
Do you know Gram Sabha is Empowered for Comprehensive Rural Development?

Empowerment of Gram Sabha	*Number of Respondents*	*Percentage*
Yes	76	63.3
No	44	36.7
Total	120	100.0

Table 6.6 reflects that 63.3 per cent respondents know this fact that Gram Sabha is empowered to undertake comprehensive rural development work, whereas 36.7 per cent respondents are not aware about this empowerment. It is evident from the above analysis that about two-thirds respondents are aware about this very important aspect of Panchayat Raj that at the grassroots level the Gram Sabha has been specially empowered.

Table 6.7

Does Gram Sabha Meeting Take Place in your Village Regularly?

Meeting of Gram Sabha	*Number of Respondents*	*Percentage*
Yes	98	81.7
No	22	18.3
Total	120	100.0

Table 6.7 emphasises that 81.7 per cent respondents confirm that regular meetings of Gram Sabhas are held in their villages. Only 18.3 per cent respondents do not feel so. It is indeed a matter of big satisfaction that more than 80 per cent respondents point out regularity of Gram Sabha meetings.

Table 6.8

If Not, Reasons

Reason	*Number of Respondents*	*Percentage*
Don't get information	11	50.0
People's apathy	05	22.7
Don't know	06	27.3
Total	22	100.0

Out of 120 selected respondents, 22 are of the view that the Gram Sabha meetings do not take place regularly. Table 6.8 interprets the reasons of non-regularity of meetings. With 11 respondents of the view that they do not get information, five respondents feel that it is due to people's apathy. Remaining six respondents do not know the reason of irregularity.

Gram Sabha Quorum

After introduction of Gram Swaraj in Madhya Pradesh, an amendment in the State Act has been done with respect to quorum. The basic assumption for the change was to have a proper and mandatory representation of all sections of society.

Table 6.9
Required Quorum for Gram Sabha Meeting

Quorum of Gram Sabha	*Number of Respondents*	*Percentage*
Right	88	73.3
Wrong	32	26.7
Total	120	100.0

As per the provisions of the Act, the quorum required for the Gram Sabha meeting is one-fifth members of the adults who have their names in the voting list of the village. Table 6.9 illustrates that 73.3 per cent respondents do know the required quorum whereas 26.7 per cent respondents do not know this fact. It is interesting to note that almost three-fourths of the respondents know this factual information. It is also important to mention here that previously the required quorum was only one-tenths members and the previous experience was that even this number was not attainable at times. In spite of the fact known to the government, quorum for Gram Sabha meetings has been enhanced which is now creating difficulties in holding meetings.

Women for Gram Sabha Quorum

Women participation through 73rd Constitution Amendment Act is a landmark decision through which 33 per cent of the seats are reserved for women. This mandatory reservation is being followed for the quorum in Gram Sabha meetings as well.

Table 6.10
Do you Know that Presence of Women is Necessary for Quorum of Gram Sabha Meeting?

Women's Presence	*Number of Respondents*	*Percentage*
Yes	79	65.8
No	41	34.2
Total	120	100.0

Table 6.10 describes that 65.8 per cent respondents know that women's presence is necessary for quorum of Gram Sabha meeting. This percentage is lower as compared to those who know the quorum required for Gram Sabha meetings.

Table 6.11

Required Number of Women for Quorum of Gram Sabha Meeting

Women Number	*Number of Respondents*	*Percentage*
Right	55	69.6
Wrong	24	30.4
Total	79	100.0

The required quorum for Gram Sabha meeting is one-third of the present members and minimum one-third of the required number for Gram Sabha quorum. Out of 79 respondents, 55 know the exact number of women required for the quorum. Though the number of respondents is slightly lower who know the required number of women for quorum, nevertheless it is a positive indication that this significant aspect of mandatory women participation is known to a considerable number.

SC/ST for Gram Sabha Quorum

After Gram Swaraj, representation of SCs/STs in Gram Sabha meetings is made mandatory in proportion to their population. Table 6.12 shows that 62.5 per cent respondents know that the

Table 6.12

Do you Know that Presence of SC/ST is Necessary for Quorum of Gram Sabha Meeting?

Know SC/ST Presence for Quorum	*Number of Respondents*	*Percentage*
Yes	75	62.5
No	45	37.5
Total	120	100.0

SC/ST presence is required for quorum. Thus, it is clear from the above mentioned table that almost two-third respondents know this fact.

Participation in Gram Sabha

Gram Sabha has always been an integral part of the concept of Gram Swaràj. Gram Sabha has been visualised as a watchdog coming between politician-bureaucratic nexus and the public at large. The important dimension of Gram Swaraj is the level of participation of people in the empowered Gram Sabha.

Table 6.13

Do you Participate in Gram Sabha Meetings?

Participation in Gram Sabha	*Number of Respondents*	*Percentage*
Regular	26	21.7
Seldom	40	33.3
Never	54	45.0
Total	120	100.0

Table 6.13 highlights the fact that 21.7 per cent respondents participate regularly in the Gram Sabha meetings, whereas 33.3 per cent respondents seldom participate in the meetings. Nearly 45 per cent respondents never participate in the meetings. Thus, it is evident from the above analysis that a significant percentage of respondents do not participate in the meetings. This is so when majority of the respondents are aware of the fact that quorum is required for Gram Sabha meeting and the presence of women and SCs/STs is mandatory.

Ninety-four respondents are of the view that they either seldom or never attend the Gram Sabha meetings and therefore it is asked as to what are the reasons of their non-participation. Table 6.14 analyses that out of 94 respondents, 52 are of the opinion that their non-participation is due to their extraordinary personal busy schedule and 20 respondents feel that they do not get information

Table 6.14
Reasons for Non-Participation

Reason	*Number of Respondents*	*Percentage*
Extraordinarily busy	52	55.3
Don't get information	20	21.3
Social taboos	13	13.8
Poor are not heard	04	04.35
Not interested	02	02.1
Groupism/casteism in panchayat	02	02.1
Meetings don't take place	01	01.0
Total	94	100.0

of the meeting. Around 13 respondents do not go to meetings because of the social taboo (females should not attend public meetings). Poor are not heard, this is cited as a reason by four respondents and two respondents equally point out the reason of non-participation as not interested and groupism/casteism in panchayat, while one respondent gives his reason that meetings do not take place. Thus, it is clear from the above analysis that the major reasons shown by the respondents are their personal work schedule, no information and social taboos.

Information about the Gram Sabha meeting is provided by chowkidar of the Gram Panchayat. Table 6.15 shows that 75 per cent respondents get that information from chowkidar. Around five per cent respondents get this information through panchayat secretary and 1.7 per cent respondents get this information from villagers, whereas 2.5 per cent respondents get this from Gram Panchayat office. Remaining 15.8 per cent respondents do not get this information at all. Thus, it is evident from the above analysis that three-fourths of the respondents get the information through the chowkidar who is assigned this responsibility. It is indeed a positive indicator that almost 85 per cent respondents get the information in time about Gram Sabha meetings.

Table 6.15

How Do You Get the Information of Gram Sabha Meeting?

Source of Information	*Number of Respondents*	*Percentage*
Chowkidar	90	75.0
Panchayat Secretary	06	05.0
Villagers	02	01.7
From Gram Panchayat office	03	02.5
Don't get information	19	15.8
Total	120	100.0

Table 6.16

When do You Get the Information of Meeting of Gram Sabha?

Time of Information	*Number of Respondents*	*Percentage*
Before one week	25	20.8
Before two days	47	39.2
Before one day	23	19.2
Same day	06	05.0
Don't get information	19	15.0
Total	120	100.0

Information of the meeting of the Gram Sabha is to be given to the members before one week. Table 6.16 explains the time of receiving the information of meeting of Gram Sabha. Only 20.8 per cent respondents get this information before one week and 39.2 per cent respondents get this information before two days, whereas 19.2 per cent respondents are informed a day before. Similarly 5 per cent respondents get this information on the same day. Remaining 15 per cent respondents do not get any information. It is clear from the above illustration that a limited number of respondents get the information within the prescribed time. However, as the village society is very close and informal, it is believed that information of this kind can be passed on from person to person as well as through the panchayat chowkidar and therefore the time of information giving is not strictly followed.

Frequency of Gram Sabha Meetings

After the implementation of Gram Swaraj in Madhya Pradesh, a provision has been made to hold the Gram Sabha meeting every month. It is complained that due to lack of quorum, Gram Sabha meetings are not held regularly and in stipulated time. Table 6.17 shows the number of meetings held in respondents' villages in the last one year. Around 26.7 per cent respondents point out that eight and above meetings are held in their villages, whereas 23.3 per cent respondents give the number of four to six meetings in a year. Only 7.5 per cent respondents are of the view that up to three meetings are held in their villages and 39.2 per cent respondents do not know the number. Rest 3.3 per cent respondents are not aware of any meeting. Thus, it is clear that a significant percentage does not know the number of meetings held during the last one year.

Table 6.17

Number of Gram Sabha Meetings Held in Last One Year

Number of Meetings	*Number of Respondents*	*Percentage*
Up to 3	09	07.5
4 to 6	28	23.3
8 and above	32	26.7
Don't know	47	39.2
No meetings	04	03.3
Total	120	100.0

Level of Presence of Different Groups in Gram Sabha Meetings

Table 6.18 indicates the level of presence of different categories/groups in Gram Sabha meetings. It is an awareness related question, which is asked to all the respondents for various groups. Scheduled Castes presence in Gram Sabha meetings is given as: almost all (17%), almost half (34.2%), very few (10.8%), don't come (4.2%) and don't know (36.7%). Female presence in Gram Sabha meetings is given as: almost half (15.8%), very few (35.8%), don't come (10.8%) and don't know 37.5%). Details about the presence of weaker sections and the poor in Gram Sabha meetings is given as: almost all (5.8%), almost half (36.7%), very few (15.8%), don't come (5%) and don't know (36.7%). Higher group presence is given as: almost all (15%), almost half (41.7%), very few (6.8%), don't come (5%) and don't know (37.5%). Presence of educated group is given as: almost all (13.3%), almost half (42.5%), very few (1.7%), don't come (5%) and don't know (37.5%) respectively.

Table 6.18

Level of Presence of Different Groups in Gram Sabha Meetings

Category	*Almost All*	*Almost Half*	*Very Few*	*Don't Come*	*Don't Know*	*Total*
Scheduled Castes	17 (14.2)	41 (34.2)	13 (10.8)	05 (4.2)	44 (36.7)	120 (100.0)
Female	00 (0.00)	19 (15.8)	43 (35.8)	13 (10.8)	45 (37.5)	120 (100.0)
Weaker sections	07 (05.8)	44 (36.7)	19 (15.8)	06 (5.0)	44 (36.7)	120 (100.0)
Higher groups	18 (15.0)	50 (41.7)	01 (00.8)	06 (5.0)	45 (37.5)	120 (100.0)
Educated groups	16 (13.3)	51 (42.5)	02 (01.7)	06 (5.0)	45 (37.5)	120 (100.0)

Figures in parentheses are percentages.

Thus, it is clear from the above analysis that more than one-third respondents do not know the level of presence of any group. Almost 15 per cent respondents feel that SC, higher caste groups and educated persons remain present in almost all the meetings. Except females, the presence of almost half in the meeting is pointed out by one-third to half of the respondents. Female group is cited maximum in the categories of very few and don't come. It denotes that maximum presence of the difference groups is in the category of almost half.

Level of Participation of Different Groups in Gram Sabha Meetings

Gram Swaraj is a form of direct democracy where it has been ensured through a mandatory provision to get the participation of all sections of the society, particularly the marginalised sections. Table 6.19 presents the level of participation of different groups.

Opinion was elicited from the respondents about the level of participation of different groups. It is interesting to note that respondents are of the opinion that educated groups (51.7%), higher groups (51.7%), SCs (31.7%), weaker sections (23.3%) and women (6.7%), participate in discussions about panchayat-related issues in Gram Sabha meetings. Respondents point out that women (26.7%), weaker sections (24.2%) and SCs (15%) sit silently. Around 45 per cent respondents equally do not know about level of participation of SC, weaker sections, educated group and higher group whereas 54.2 per cent respondents do not know about the participation of women in Gram Sabha meetings.

Table 6.19

Level of Participation of Different Groups in Gram Sabha Meetings

Category	*Discuss Issues*	*Sit Silently*	*Only make Signatures*	*Don't Know*	*Total*
Scheduled Castes	38 (31.7)	18 (15.0)	10 (8.3)	54 (45.0)	120 (100.0)
Women	08 (06.7)	32 (26.7)	15 (12.5)	65 (54.2)	120 (100.0)
Weaker sections	28 (23.3)	29 (24.2)	09 (07.5)	54 (45.0)	120 (100.0)
Educated groups	62 (51.7)	03 (02.5)	01 (00.8)	54 (45.0)	120 (100.0)
Higher groups	62 (51.7)	03 (02.5)	01 (00.8)	54 (45.0)	120 (100.0)

Figures in parentheses are percentages.

The above analysis clearly depicts that only the educated and higher groups remain active in Gram Sabha discussions while SC, women and weaker sections sit silently.

Table 6.20

Reasons of Absence

Reason	*Number of Respondents*	*Percentage*
Scheduled Castes		
Don't get information	01	00.8
Nobody listens	03	02.5
Don't know	05	04.2
Personal reasons	09	07.5
Female		
Social evils	34	28.3
Personal reasons	09	07.5
Don't get information	02	01.7
Don't know	07	05.8
Nobody listens	01	00.8
Weaker Section/Poor		
Don't get information	02	01.7
Nobody listens	04	03.3
Personal work	14	11.7
Illiteracy	01	00.8
Don't know	04	03.3
Higher Group		
Nobody listens	02	01.7
Don't know	05	04.2
Educated Group		
Don't know	06	05.0
Don't take interest	03	02.5

Table 6.20 provides the reasons for the absence of different groups in Gram Sabha meeting. The reasons for the absence of Scheduled Castes are personal reasons (9), do not know (5), nobody listens (3) and do not get timely information (1). Reasons

for the absence of females are social evils (34), personal reasons (9), don't know (7), don't get information (2) and nobody listens (1). Reasons for the absence of weaker sections/poor are personal work (14), nobody listens (4), don't know (4), don't get information (2) and illiteracy (1). Reasons for the absence of higher group are – don't know (5) and nobody listens (2). Reasons for the absence of educated groups are don't know (6) and don't take interest (3). Thus, the reasons of absence clearly show that in majority cases it is due to personal reasons but in the case of the females it is due to social evils.

Issues of Discussion in Gram Sabha Meeting

Gram Sabha has now been empowered to take all decisions for the overall development of the village. Table 6.21 reflects prominent issues discussed in Gram Sabha meetings. Whereas 26.7 per cent respondents point out that social problems are discussed, 10.8 per cent respondents feel that the selection of beneficiaries is discussed. While 2.5 per cent respondents point out that school related matters are discussed, 11.7 per cent respondents discuss all these three issues cited above. Finally, 5.8 per cent respondents feel that there is no issue for discussion.

Table 6.21

Issues for Discussion in Gram Sabha Meeting

Issues	*Number of Respondents*	*Percentage*
Related to local problems	32	26.7
Related to school	03	02.5
Selection of beneficiaries for schemes	13	10.8
All above	14	11.7
No issue	07	05.8
Don't know	51	42.5
Total	120	100.0

It is clear from the answers that only local problems are the main issues of discussion. It is indeed a matter of concern that 42.5

per cent members are unaware about the issues discussed in Gram Sabha. Presumably this is due to their rural background and illiteracy.

Decision-making Process

It is indeed a matter of serious concern as how decisions are taken in the Gram Sabha meetings. Table 6.22 explains how decisions are arrived at in Gram Sabha meetings. Around 41.7 per cent respondents are of the opinion that decisions are taken unanimously; 14.1 per cent respondents point out that the decisions are taken as per the wishes of the Sarpanch or panchayat representatives; 42.5 per cent respondents do not know about this, whereas 1.7 per cent respondents are of the view that as there are no meetings, the question of decision-making does not arise here.

It is clear from the above analysis that a sizeable number of respondents have expressed their views that the decisions are unanimous. At the same time almost equal number of respondents do not know about decision taking process but even then it confirms that slowly and gradually people are getting closer to the issues of panchayats.

Table 6.22

How are the Decisions Taken on Issues in Gram Sabha Meeting?

Decision on Issues	*Number of Respondents*	*Percentage*
Unanimously	50	41.7
As per the wish of Sarpanch or panchayat representatives	17	14.1
Don't know	51	42.5
No meeting	02	01.7
Total	120	100.0

Raising Viewpoint in Gram Sabha Meeting

Table 6.23 reflects the views expressed by respondents in the Gram Sabha meetings. Out of 120 respondents, 28 express their views whereas 92 respondents never raised any issue. Out of the 28 respondents who had raised their viewpoint in Gram Sabha, 14 of them were related to infrastructural development; seven to construction work and the remaining seven respondents took the initiative to pursue their self-related matters.

Table 6.23

Have you Raised your Viewpoint on any Issue in Gram Sabha Meeting?

Views Raised	*Number of Respondents*	*Percentage*
Infrastructure related	14	50.0
Construction work related	07	25.0
Individuals benefit related	07	25.0
Total	28	100.0

Table 6.24 interprets the reasons as to why some respondents do not raise any issue in Gram Panchayat meetings. Out of 120 respondents, 92 respondents do not raise any issue in Gram Sabha meeting. As many as 44 respondents point out the reason for not raising any issue, as they do not go to meetings. While 28 respondents feel that they do not require it, the reason nobody listens is given by seven respondents. Five respondents do not know how to

Table 6.24

Reasons for not Raising Issues

Reason	*Number of Respondents*	*Percentage*
Not required	28	30.4
Irregular meetings	01	01.1
Nobody listens	07	07.7
No information	03	03.3
Don't go to meetings	44	47.8
Don't get information	02	02.2
Hesitate to speak out	02	02.2
Don't know	05	05.4
Total	92	100.0

raise issues whereas another five respondents show the reason, as they do not get information of meetings. Two respondents do not raise issues because they hesitate to speak out. The remaining single respondent makes a view that the meetings are irregular.

Thus, it is clear from the analysis that majority of the respondents do not raise issues since they do not go to meetings, whereas a significant number do not require it.

Unanimity of Decisions in Gram Sabha

It is very important and pertinent to know the decision-making process in Gram Sabha meetings. Table 6.25 illustrates the unanimity of decisions in Gram Sabha. While 49.2 per cent respondents are of the view that the decisions are unanimous, 25.8 per cent respondents feel that the decision taken in the Gram Sabha meetings are not unanimous. Remaining 25 per cent respondents do not know whether the decisions taken by Gram Sabha are unanimous. It is a positive indication that almost half of the respondents are of the view that the decisions are unanimous.

Table 6.25

Are the Decisions Unanimously Taken in Gram Sabha?

Decision Unanimous	*Number of Respondents*	*Percentage*
Yes	59	49.2
No	31	25.8
Don't know	30	25.0
Total	120	100.0

Table 6.26 describes the bases of decisions in the cases where decisions are not unanimous. Out of 31 respondents who have argued that the decisions are not unanimous, 16 respondents point out that the decisions are taken on the advise of influential people; 11 respondents feel that the decisions are taken as per the wish of Sarpanch; and two respondents are of the view that the decisions are taken on the basis of region. Here, region stands for the ward and representation of different groups in panchayats from different *mohallas*. Remaining two respondents do not know the bases of

taking decisions. Thus, it is evident from the above analysis that influential people and Sarpanch continue to influence the decision-making process in Gram Sabha meeting.

Table 6.26

If Not, the Basis of Decisions

Basis	*Number of Respondents*	*Percentage*
On the advise of influential people	16	51.5
On the basis of region	02	06.5
As per the wish of Sarpanch	11	35.5
Don't know	02	06.5
Total	31	100.0

Problems Existing in Village

Infrastructure and basic amenities are still continuing as major problems in the rural areas. Despite all efforts, the government from centre and state could not make a significant change in this sphere. After the 73rd Amendment Act all this responsibilities are shouldered by the panchayats.

Table 6.27

Are the Following Problems Existing in your Village?

Problems	*Yes*	*No*	*Don't know*	*Total*
Drinking water	40 (33.3)	79 (65.8)	01 (00.8)	120 (100)
Approach road	77 (64.2)	42 (35.0)	01(00.8)	120 (100)
Drainage	84 (70.0)	35 (29.2)	01(00.8)	120 (100)
Irrigation	31 (25.8)	87 (72.5)	02 (01.7)	120 (100)
Electricity	106 (88.3)	14 (11.7)	00 (00.0)	120 (100)
Encroachment	55 (45.8)	64 (53.3)	01(00.8)	120 (100)
Employment	80 (66.7)	39 (32.5)	01(00.8)	120 (100)
Education	64 (53.3)	54 (45.0)	02 (01.7)	120 (100)
Health	73 (60.8)	46 (38.3)	01(00.8)	120 (100)
Communication	56 (46.7)	63 (52.5)	01(00.8)	120 (100)

Figures in parentheses are percentages.

Table 6.27 highlights the problems in the village. Problems cited by the respondents are given as: drinking water (33.3%), approach road (64.2%), drainage (70%), irrigation (25.8%), electricity (88.3%), encroachment (45.8%), employment (66.7%), education (53.3%), health (60.8%) and communication (46.7%).

Thus, it is clear from the above analysis that 10 problems were identified and in all cases the respondents were clear about their views. Only one or two respondents do not know about the problems. Electricity, drainage and employment are considered as problems by majority respondents.

Table 6.28

Have you Raised These Problems in Gram Sabha?

Answer	*Number of Respondents*	*Percentage*
Yes	18	15.0
No	102	85.0
Total	120	100.0

It is really important from the point that a significant number of respondents know the problems of the village. Table 6.28 makes an attempt to know as to whether these problems were raised in Gram Sabha meetings. According to only 15 per cent respondents these problems have been raised in the Gram Sabha meetings whereas 85 per cent respondents have not raised these problems in the Gram Sabha meetings. It is clear from the above interpretation that the number of respondents who have raised any problem in the Gram Sabha meetings is very limited. On the contrary, majority of respondents know the prevailing problems at the village level.

Table 6.29 illustrates the responses to the problems raised in Gram Sabha meetings. Out of 18 respondents, six respondents are of the view that nothing happened; five respondents point out that some work started and stopped; three respondents feel that only proposal passed; and two respondents equally clarify that attention was not given and assurance was given. It is very clear that the

Table 6.29

If Yes, What was the Response to Problem?

Response	*Number of Respondents*	*Percentage*
Nothing happened	06	33.3
Attention not given	02	11.1
Some work started and stopped	05	27.8
Only proposal passed	03	16.7
Assurance given	02	11.1
Total	18	100.0

response to the problems is of a mixed nature. In fact, if any issue is raised in Gram Sabha meeting, it has to be discussed threadbare and then some appropriate proposal is to be forwarded to the concerned agencies. It is therefore very obvious to get such responses to the problem.

Work Done by Panchayat

Basically to know the works done by panchayat through villagers is to assess their understanding for panchayat work. After Gram Swaraj the expected involvement of villagers is much higher. The concept of social audit can only be brought into practice, if the villagers are well versed with the work done by the panchayats.

Table 6.30 describes the details of the work done by the panchayat. Inspection of school – never done (25%), one-two time (10%), regularly (30.8%) and don't know (34.2%). Repair and maintenance of school building – never done (18.3%), one-two time (23.3%), regularly (26.7%) and don't know (31.7%). Inspection of health facilities – never done (15.8%), one-two time (28.3%), regularly (19.2%) and don't know (36.7%). Camps of family planning – never done (20%), one-two time (40.8%), regularly (4.2%) and don't know (35%). Construction and repairs of road – never done (25.8%), one-two time (37.5%), regularly (13.3%) and don't know (23.7%). Drainage construction – never done (14.2%), one-two time (48.3%), regularly (14.2%) and don't know (23.3%). Drinking water facilities – never done (11.7%), one-two time (16.7%), regularly (46.7%) and don't know (25%).

Table 6.30
Work Done by Panchayat

Work	*Never done*	*One-Two times*	*Regularly*	*Don't know*	*Total*
Inspection of school	30 (25.0)	12 (10.0)	37 (30.8)	41 (34.2)	120 (100)
Repair and maintenance of school building	22 (18.3)	28 (23.3)	32 (26.7)	38 (31 7)	120 (100)
Inspection of health facilities	19 (15.8)	34 (28.3)	23 (19.2)	44 (36.7)	120 (100)
Camps of family planning	24 (20.0)	49(40.8)	05 (04.2)	42 (35.0)	120 (100)
Construction and repairs of roads	31 (25.8)	45 (37.5)	16 (13.3)	28 (23.3)	120 (100)
Drainage construction	17 (14.2)	58 (48.3)	17 (14.2)	28 (23.3)	120 (100)
Drinking water facility	14 (11.7)	20 (16.7)	56 (46.7)	30 (25.0)	120 (100)
Irrigation	13 (10.8)	36 (30.0)	32 (26.7)	39 (32.5)	120 (100)
Agricultural extension	12 (10.0)	44 (36.7)	21 (17.5)	43 (35.8)	120 (100)
Employment generation	23 (19.2)	49 (40.8)	05 (04.2)	43 (35.8)	120 (100)
Economic help	24 (20.0)	41 (34.2)	06 (05.0)	49 (40.8)	120 (100)
Cooperation in house construction	16 (13.3)	51 (42.5)	03 (02.5)	50 (41.7)	120 (100)
Security	12 (10.0)	40 (33.3)	12 (10.0)	56 (46.7)	120 (100)
Arrangements for social/ religious functions	09 (07.5)	49 (40.8)	05 (04.2)	57 (47.5)	120 (100)
Old age pension	13 (10.8)	30 (25.0)	31 (25.8)	46 (38.3)	120 (100)

Figures in parentheses are percentages.

Irrigation – never done (10.8%), one-two time (30%), regularly (26.7%) and don't know (32.5%). Agriculture extension – never done (1%), one-two time (36.7%), regularly (17.5%) and don't know (35.8%). Employment generation – never done (17.2%), one-two time (40.8%), regularly (4.2%) and don't know (35.8%). Economic help – never done (20%), one-two time (34.2%), regularly (5%) and don't know (40.8%). Cooperation in house construction – never done (13.3%), one-two time (42.5%), regularly (2.5%) and don't know (41.7%). Security – never done

(10%), one-two time (33.3%), regularly (10.6%) and don't know (46.7%). Arrangements for social/religious function – never done (7.5%), one-two time (40.8%), regularly (4.2%) and don't know (47.5%). Old age pension – never done (10.8%), one-two time (25%), regularly (25.8%) and don't know (38.3%).

Thus, this detailed elaboration gives a fair picture of work done by the panchayat from the point of view of villagers. It is a positive indication that in majority cases almost all works were either done one-two times or regularly by panchayat whereas a considerable number do not know. Looking into the village clientele's exposure and understanding, it is indeed a step forward that people are taking grips over the functional issues of panchayat.

Committee System in Gram Swaraj

The most important innovation introduced through Gram Swaraj is the committee system. The basic idea behind having different committees is to ascertain the participation of different groups particularly the stakeholders. Assigning work to different committees brings in efficiency and location of responsibility in panchayat working. It is also a mode of division of labour and ensuring work input from panchayat meetings.

Table 6.31

Do you Know About the Committee System in Gram Swaraj?

Answer	*Number of Respondents*	*Percentage*
Yes	49	40.8
No	71	59.2
Total	120	100.0

Table 6.31 describes about the knowledge of committee system in Gram Swaraj. Whereas 40.8 per cent respondents know the committee system. Remaining 59.2 per cent respondents do not know about the committee system in Gram Swaraj. It suggests that majority respondents do not know the committee system.

Table 6.32

If Yes, Whether these Committees are Formed in your Village?

Committees Formed	*Yes*	*No*	*Total*
Village Development Committee	49 (100.0)	00 (0.0)	49 (100.0)
Community Resources Committee	41 (83.7)	08 (06.3)	49 (100.0)
Agriculture Committee	47 (95.9)	02 (04.1)	49 (100.0)
Health Committee	47 (95.9)	02 (04.1)	49 (100.0)
Village Security Committee	49 (100.0)	00 (0.0)	49 (100.0)
Infrastructure Committee	43 (87.7)	06 (12.3)	49 (100.0)
Education Committee	49 (100.0)	00 (0.0)	49 (100.0)
Social Justice Committee	47 (95.9)	02 (04.1)	49 (100.0)

Figures in parentheses are percentages.

Table 6.32 shows the information related to formation of various committees. Eight committees are formed in each village to look after the overall activities of the village. Out of 49 respondents, who were aware about the committee system, answered their understanding towards different committees.

In response to the question whether these committees are formed in your village, the committee-wise response is as follows: Village Development Committee (49), Community Resource Committee (41), Agriculture Committee (47), Health Committee (47), Village Security Committee (49), Infrastructure Committee (43), Education Committee (49), Social Justice Committee (47). Thus, it is very clear from the responses that most of the respondents who are aware about the committees know about the various committees' formation.

Works of Different Committees

Table 6.33 reveals the works done by different committees. According to respondents who know about the different committees elaborate the works. Village Development Committee has done – solve the water problem (2), Kharanja construction (11), road construction (3), village development (14), don't know

(19). Community Resource Committee has done – conservation of natural resources (6), tank construction (1), maintenance of government buildings (2), no work (3), don't know (37). Agriculture committee has done – solve the water problem (2), make available fertilizer and seeds (14), Improve agriculture (12), don't know (21). Health Committee has done – hospital management (8), make available medicines (2), health check-ups (18), don't know (21). Village Security Committee has done – security of village (25), cooperate in arresting criminals (1), don't know (23). Infrastructure Committee has done – solve the problems of school (10), total development of the village (3), road construction (2), conservation of forest (1), don't know (33). Education Committee has done – maintenance and construction of school (5), make available teachers (8), inspire parents to send children to school (1), inspect school (12), don't know (23). Social Justice Committee has done – prevent the disputes in village (25), stop partiality (2), don't know (22).

This explanation clearly confirms that still a major chunk of the respondents do not know about the specific works of specific committees. Nevertheless a sizeable number has given specific works, which is of significant importance from the point of view of Gram Swaraj system.

Table 6.33

Works of Different Committees

Works	*Number of Respondents*	*Percentage*
Village Development Committee		
Solve the water problem	02	01.7
Kharanja construction	11	09.2
Road construction	03	02.5
Village development	14	11.7
Don't know	19	15.8
Community Resources Committee		
Conservation of natural resources	06	12.2

Contd...

Contd...

Tank construction	01	02.1
Maintenance of government buildings	02	04.1
No work	03	06.1
Don't know	37	75.5
Agriculture Committee		
Solve the water problem	02	04.1
Make available fertiliser and seeds	14	28.6
Improve agriculture	12	24.5
Don't know	21	42.8
Health Committee		
Hospital management	08	16.3
Make available medicines	02	04.1
Health check-ups	18	36.7
Don't know	21	42.8
Village Security Committee		
Security of village	25	51.0
Cooperate in arresting criminals	01	02.1
Don't know	23	46.9
Infrastructure Committee		
Solve the problems of school	10	20.4
Total development of the village	03	06.1
Road construction	02	04.1
Conservation of forest	01	02.1
Don't know	33	67.3
Education Committee		
Maintenance and Construction of school	05	10.2
Make available teachers	08	16.4
Inspire parents to send children to school	01	02.1
Inspect school	12	20.4
Don't know	23	46.9
Social Justice Committee		
Prevent the disputes in village	25	51.0
Stop partiality	02	04.2
Don't know	22	44.8

Formation of Committees

Gram Swaraj system has a special feature of committee system. A procedure has been laid down in the rules to form the committees, like the members and chairperson will be elected in first Gram Sabha meeting after the enactment of Gram Swaraj. Stakeholders should be made members of the committees. Due representation of marginalised section of the society is to be ensured.

Table 6.34

How Committees are Formed?

Formation of Committees	*Number of Respondents*	*Percentage*
As per the wish of Sarpanch	06	05.0
Unanimous nomination in Gram Sabha	41	34.2
Don't know	73	60.8
Total	120	100.0

Table 6.34 reflects the procedure of formation of committees. While 34.2 per cent respondents are of the view that it is done through unanimous nomination in Gram Sabha, 5 per cent respondents point out that it is done as per the wish of Sarpanch. Remaining 60.8 per cent respondents do not know the procedure of formation of committees. It clearly confirms that majority respondents are not familiar with the committee formation procedure. Nevertheless, one-third respondents provide the right procedure of formation, which is a positive indication.

Table 6.35

Are You a Member of Any Committee?

Answer	*Number of Respondents*	*Percentage*
Yes	53	44.2
No	67	55.8
Total	120	100.0

Table 6.35 illustrates the respondents' membership of any committee. While 44.2 per cent respondents opine that they are members of the committees, remaining 55.8 per cent respondents are not members of any committee.

Thus, it is evident from the above analysis that almost half of the selected respondents are members in various committees. It shows that through committee system maximum villagers are directly associated with the implementation of Gram Swaraj.

Table 6.36

If Yes, Which Committee?

Committee	*Number of Respondents*	*Percentage*
Village Development Committee	02	03.8
Education Committee	07	13.7
Social Justice Committee	05	09.4
Village Security Committee	09	17.0
Agriculture Committee	06	11.3
Community Resources Committee	06	11.3
Health Committee	07	13.2
Infrastructure Committee	03	05.7
Don't know	08	15.1
Total	53	100.0

Table 6.36 describes the membership of a particular committee of the respondents. Out of 53 respondents those are members have given the details as mentioned below: village education committee (2), education committee (7), social justice committee (5), village security committee (9), agriculture committee (6), community resources committee (6), health committee (7), infrastructure committee (3), remaining 8 respondents do not know the name of committee of which they are members. It clearly provides a fair picture that the selected respondents represent almost all committees. A small number is not aware about the name of the specific committee regarding their membership.

Consideration of Decisions of Committees in Gram Sabha

The basic idea behind having different committees is to have a decentralised pattern of decision-making. It provides ample opportunity to villagers particularly the representatives of marginalised section of the society and stakeholders to take part in committee meetings and raise their voice on the issues of greater interest for all.

Table 6.37

How are the Decisions of Committees Considered in Gram Sabha Meeting?

Decision	*Number of Respondents*	*Percentage*
Unanimous decision with consent	50	41.7
Sarpanch takes decision on his own	10	08.3
Don't go to meeting	24	20.0
No meeting	05	04.2
Don't know	31	25.8
Total	120	100.0

Table 6.37 highlights the consideration of decisions of committees in Gram Sabha meetings. While 41.7 per cent respondents are of the view that the decisions are unanimous with mutual consent, 20 per cent respondents point out that they do not go to meetings. Whereas 8.3 per cent respondents argue that Sarpanch takes decision on his own, 4.2 per cent respondents feel that there is no meeting and remaining 25.8 per cent respondents do not know about this. Thus, it can be inferred that maximum respondents are favouring unanimous decision-making with mutual consent. Almost one-fourths do not know about this. Looking into the innovation and its technicality, a sizeable number is coming closer to understanding the system.

Awareness about Panchayat-Related Individuals

At village level, the Gram Sabha members are directly involved in various activities of panchayat. They come in contact with many individuals and looking into this aspect a question was asked to respondents regarding their knowledge.

Table 6.38 illustrates the details in this regard. The following individuals are known to the number of respondent given in bracket – Sarpanch (117), Up-sarpanch (107), Koshadhyaksha (95), Panchayat Secretary (100), Stakeholders (12), Janpad Panchayat CEO (32), Zilla Panchayat CEO (27) and Collector (32).

Table 6.38

Do you know the Following Individuals?

Know	*Yes*	*No*	*Total*
Sarpanch	117 (97.5)	03 (02.5)	120 (100.0)
Up-sarpanch	107 (89.2)	13 (10.8)	120 (100.0)
Koshadhyaksha	95 (79.2)	25 (20.8)	120 (100.0)
Panchayat Secretary	100 (83.3)	20 (16.7)	120 (100.0)
Stake Holder	12 (10.0)	108 (90.0)	120 (100.0)
Janpad Panchayat CEO	32 (26.7)	88 (73.3)	120 (100.0)
Zilla Panchayat CEO	27 (22.5)	93 (77.5)	120 (100.0)
Collector	32 (26.7)	88 (73.3)	120 (100.0)

Figures in parentheses are percentages.

Thus, it is clear from the above analysis that the village level individuals are known to maximum respondents, whereas the Janpad and district level officials are also known to almost one-third respondents. The least known individual is the stake-holder. It is due to the fact that first, it is a new concept which emerged out with Gram Swaraj and second, people are not well versed with this inclusion of stakeholder in the various committees.

Gram Kosh

Historically speaking, the Gram Kosh is a very old time-effective system at the village level. After a passage of time this institution was out of practice in villages. Looking into the rich legacy and vibrancy of such system it has been revived through Gram Swaraj.

Table 6.39

Whether Gram Kosh is Established in your Village?

Answer	*Number of Respondents*	*Percentage*
Yes	17	14.2
No	101	84.2
Don't Know	02	01.7
Total	120	100.0

Table 6.39 explains the establishment of Gram Kosh in villages. Only 14.2 per cent respondents say that Gram Kosh has been established in their villages under the new system whereas 84.2 per cent respondents say 'No'. Remaining two respondents do not know about this. It is thus clear that one very important aspect of Gram Swaraj is not seriously taken into consideration. The obvious reason for such poor response is lack of information regarding Gram Kosh and its functioning utility among villagers.

The Gram Kosh includes four components – Anna kosh, Shram kosh, Vastu kosh and Nagad kosh. Out of 17 respondents those know about the establishment of Gram Kosh have given the details of four different kosh in Table 6.40.

Table 6.40

Do You Know the Following Kosh?

Answer	*Know*	*Don't Know*	*Total*
Anna Kosh	06 (35.3)	11 (64.7)	17 (100.0)
Shram Kosh	03 (17.6)	14 (82.4)	17 (100.0)
Vastu Kosh	03 (17.6)	14 (82.4)	17 (100.0)
Nagad Kosh	10 (58.8)	07 (41.2)	17 (100.0)

Figures in parentheses are percentages.

Anna Kosh is known to six respondents. Shram Kosh is known to three respondents and three respondents know the Vastu Kosh. Nagad Kosh is known to ten respondents. Thus, it is clear that a very limited number know the Gram Kosh and out of them a small number know the various koshas under Gram Kosh.

Koshadhyaksha (Treasurer) in Gram Swaraj

The office of Koshadhyaksha (Treasurer) has been a controversial one in the working system of Gram Swaraj. It has been argued by Sarpanch and his coterie that the creation of the post of koshadhyaksha is to undermine the position of Sarpanch. Though the funds available at the Gram Panchayat level are very limited and all these funds are to be utilised with the consent of Gram Sabha but the post of Koshadhyaksha has remained bone of contention at occasions due to fund utilization issue.

Table 6.41 throws light on the election procedure of Koshadhyaksha. Whereas 70.8 per cent respondents were of the view that the election was unanimous, 5.8 per cent respondents point out that it was by voting. Around 4.2 per cent respondents present the fact that it was on the advise of PR representatives and 1.7 per cent respondents equally argued that it was on the basis of caste and it was done on the advise of local politician. Remaining 15.8 per cent respondents did not know the procedure. This shows that majority of respondents were in favour of unanimous election.

Table 6.41

Election of Koshadhyaksha

Basis of Election	*Number of Respondents*	*Percentage*
Unanimous	85	70.8
On the basis of caste	02	01.7
On the advise of local politician	02	01.7
On the advise of PR representatives	05	04.2
By voting	07	05.8
Don't know	19	15.8
Total	120	100.0

Last Work Done by Panchayat

Empowerment of Gram Sabha is basically to have maximum participation of people in the decision-making and in all other employment activities. The concept of social audit is also very important from the point of view of awareness of Gram Sabha members towards the work done by panchayat.

Table 6.42 describes the understanding of Gram Sabha members for the last work done by panchayat. Nearly 25 per cent respondents know the name of the work; 19.2 per cent respondents know the cost of the work; 19.2 per cent respondents know the allotment received; 18.3 per cent respondents know the total expenditure done on the work; 22.5 per cent respondents know the period of work; 22.5 per cent respondents know the quality of construction material; and 22.5 per cent respondents know the construction agency.

Table 6.42

Do You Know the Last Work Done by Panchayat?

Work Done	*Know*	*Don't Know*	*Total*
Work name	30 (25.0)	90 (75.0)	120 (100.0)
Cost of work	23 (19.2)	97 (80.8)	120 (100.0)
Allotment received	23 (19.2)	97 (80.8)	120 (100.0)
Total expenditure	22 (18.3)	98 (81.7)	120 (100.0)
Period	27 (22.5)	93 (77.5)	120 (100.0)
Quality of construction material	27 (22.5)	93 (77.5)	120 (100.0)
Agency	27 (22.5)	93 (77.5)	120 (100.0)

Figures in parentheses are percentages.

Thus, it is clear from the above description that the various facts of the work done by panchayat are known to one-fourth or below percentage of respondents. Looking at the technicality of the issue, it is a welcome sign.

Role of Sarpanch after Gram Swaraj

After 73rd Amendment, Madhya Pradesh government took initiatives and introduced Panchayat Raj. The PRIs were given enormous powers to look into the multi-faceted task of rural development. The Sarpanch in the new system started exercising all the powers on his own. A threat was seen that this Panchayat Raj might become Sarpanch Raj. The State Government, against this backdrop, introduced Gram Swaraj and made Gram Sabha, the hub of all activities.

Table 6.43

After Gram Swaraj the Role of Sarpanch is Changed

Changing Role of Sarpanch	*Number of Respondents*	*Percentage*
Sarpanch takes decisions unanimously	37	30.8
Committee system lowered the burden of Sarpanch	03	02.5
No difference/Sarpanch's monopoly	64	53.4

Table 6.43 reflects the changing role of Sarpanch after Gram Swaraj. Around 30.8 per cent respondents are of the view that the Sarpanch takes decisions unanimously and 2.5 per cent respondents point out that committee system lowered the burden of Sarpanch. On the contrary, 53.4 per cent respondents still feel that there is no difference; Sarpanch has monopoly. Remaining 13.3 per cent respondents do not know. Thus, it is clear that almost one-third respondents have witnessed the positive change, whereas more than half of the respondents find no difference in the role.

Response of Rural Elites

Village society is different one and it has strong feudal characteristics even after more than five decades of independence. Rural elites have been playing vital and judgmental roles in the villages.

Table 6.44 observes the attitude of rural elite in local developmental issues. A good 80 per cent respondents are of the view that they have cooperative attitude and take interest in development works; 3.3 per cent respondents point out that they do not listen to anybody; 10.8 per cent respondents opine that they are not cooperative; 1.7 per cent respondents equally argue that they fight for hegemony and there is no change. Remaining 2.5 per cent respondents do not know about it. Thus, it is clear that overwhelming majority of the respondents cite cooperative attitude, which has special meaning from the point of view of rural socio-economic disparities and hegemonic situations of a few.

Table 6.44

How are Rural Elites Cooperating in Local Developmental Issues?

Help of Rural Elite	*Number of Respondents*	*Percentage*
Cooperative attitude and take interest in development works	96	80.0
Don't listen to anybody	04	03.3
Fight for hegemony	02	01.7
No change	02	01.7
No cooperation	13	10.8
Don't know	03	02.5
Total	120	100.0

Attitude of Panchayat Representatives and Officials

Gram Sabha's expanded role and its revival has special significance from the point of view of attitude of panchayat representatives and officials.

Table 6.45

What is the Attitude of Panchayat Representatives and Officials Towards Gram Sabha?

PRR and Officials Attitude	*Number of Respondents*	*Percentage*
Good and cooperative attitude	90	75.0
Bad behaviour	08	06.7
No cooperation	02	01.7
Both are corrupt	01	00.8
Don't know	19	15.8
Total	120	100.0

Table 6.45 interprets the attitude of panchayat representatives and officials towards Gram Sabha. As many as 75 per cent respondents are of the view that their attitude is good and cooperative; 6.7 per cent respondents point out it as bad behaviour; 1.7 per cent respondents feel that they are not cooperative; and one respondent argues it, as both are corrupt. Remaining 15.8 per cent respondents

do not know about it. Thus, it can be stated that three-fourths of the respondents find their attitude good and cooperative which is really very important for the smooth functioning of the Gram Sabha.

Changes due to Gram Swaraj

Table 6.46 describes the changes discernible due to Gram Swaraj. Around 35 per cent respondents find that development works are completed; 3.3 per cent respondents feel that people's participation is increased; 9.2 per cent respondents are of the view that village problems are carried out; 48.3 per cent respondents point out that there is no change; and 2.5 per cent respondents argue that development works are lowered, whereas 1.7 per cent respondents do not know.

Table 6.46

What Kind of Change is Discernible due to Gram Swaraj?

Changes	*Number of Respondents*	*Percentage*
Development works are completed	44	35.0
People's participation increased	04	03.3
Village problems are carried out	11	09.2
No change	58	48.3
Poor are unheard	01	00.8
Development works are lowered	03	02.5
Don't know	02	01.7

Thus, it is clear from the above analysis that almost half of the respondents do not find any change due to Gram Swaraj whereas more than one-third respondents see positive change.

Difference due to Gram Swaraj

Table 6.47 compares the difference in the system after Gram Swaraj. Nearly 22.5 per cent respondents are of the view that now all people come together with consensus for works; 9.2 per cent respondents feel that now the development works are done on time and more in number; 5.8 per cent respondents point out that villagers are provided more powers; 5 per cent respondents argue that previously works were completed easily but not now; 3.3 per cent respondents find that people do not know about rights; 44.2 per cent respondents are of the view that there is no difference; and 9.2 per cent respondents do not know about the difference. Thus, it is clear that significant number could provide the positive difference. At the same time a remarkable number do not find any difference. In fact it is all because at the grassroots level people are not made aware of the system.

Table 6.47

What is the Difference Now Than Before in the System?

Change	*Number of Respondents*	*Percentage*
Now all people come together with consensus for works	27	22.5
Now the development works are done on time and are more in number	11	09.2
Previously works were completed easily, but not now	06	05.0
Villagers are provided more powers	07	05.8
People don't know about rights	04	03.3
No difference	53	44.2
Don't know	11	09.2

Deciding Role of Weaker Sections

The amendment in Madhya Pradesh Panchayat Raj Act, 1993 in 2001 for Gram Swaraj has taken special care for the decisive role of weaker sections of society. Participation of weaker sections in the process of decision-making is ensured.

Table 6.48

After Gram Swaraj is the Weaker Section's Role Decisive?

Answer	*Number of Respondents*	*Percentage*
Yes	40	33.3
No	80	66.7
Total	120	100.0

Table 6.48 clarifies the respondents' opinion regarding decisive role of the weaker section. As many as 33.3 per cent respondents are of the view that the weaker section has a decisive role, whereas remaining do not think so. Thus, it is clear from the above interpretation that one-third respondents have recognised the role as decisive. It is quite obvious that the amendment package has many special dimensions for the participation of weaker section but since this new phenomenon has not yet been properly disseminated to the masses, in such a circumstances the percentage saying 'yes' is very encouraging.

Table 6.49
If Yes, How?

Role	*Number of Respondents*	*Percentage*
Now poor and lower class people also project problems	25	62.5
All issues are discussed	07	17.5
All have a decisive role	05	12.5
Don't know	03	07.5
Total	40	100.0

Out of 40 respondents those have said, that the weaker section has a decisive role, were questioned about the role. As many as 25 respondents feel that now poor and lower class people also project problems; seven respondents are of the view that all issues are discussed; five respondents point out that all have a decisive role, whereas three respondents say that they do not know. Thus, it is indeed significant that weaker section has active participation in process.

Problems in the Functioning of Gram Swaraj

Table 6.50 illustrates the problems in the functioning of Gram Swaraj. A group of 23.3 per cent respondents feel that the prominent problem in the functioning is social evils/traditional problems; 5.8 per cent respondents point out the problem of funds;

4.2 per cent respondents are of the view that Sarpanch, officials, representatives do not listen; and 1.7 per cent respondents complain of not getting information. Corruption as a problem is cited by two respondents; 7.5 per cent respondents feel that there is a lack of awareness; 5.8 per cent respondents argue that there is a problem of quorum; 3.3 per cent respondents cite the problem of panchayat building. Unawareness of Sarpanch is referred as problem by 1.7 per cent respondents and 17.5 per cent respondents do not find any problem, whereas 35 per cent respondents do not know any problem. In fact, due to lack of exposure and understanding of the Gram Swaraj the number of persons acquainted with the problem are very limited but nevertheless respondents cite all possible problems.

Table 6.50

Problems in the Functioning of Gram Swaraj

Problems	*Number of Respondents*	*Percentage*
Social evils/traditional problems	28	23.3
Problem of fund	07	05.8
Sarpanch, officials, representatives don't listen	05	04.2
Don't get information	02	01.7
Corruption	02	01.7
Lack of awareness	09	07.5
Problem of quorum	07	05.8
Problem of panchayat building	04	03.3
Sarpanch is not aware	02	01.7
No problem	21	17.5
Don't know	42	35.0

Suggestions to Improve the Gram Swaraj System

Table 6.51 provides suggestions to improve the Gram Swaraj system. Around 21.7 per cent respondents are of the view that people should be made aware; 9.2 per cent respondents point out that problem of fund should be solved; 3.3 per cent respondents feel that committees should be given maximum powers; 2.5 per cent respondents argue that information related to income/expenditure should be made public; 5.8 per cent respondents suggest that poor should be given more powers/poor should be listened first; 10.8 per cent respondents are of the view that women's problem should be solved; 4.2 per cent respondents point out that information given should be made compulsory; 9.2 per cent respondents argue that Gram Sabha should be empowered with more powers; 6.7 per cent respondents feel that people should be educated; three respondents equally suggest that sarpanch should be given more power and Sarpanch's power should be curtailed; 2.5 per cent respondents feel that everybody should come in Gram Sabha; and 35 per cent respondents do not have any suggestions.

Table 6.51

Suggestions to Improve the Gram Swaraj System

Suggestion	*Number of Respondents*	*Percentage*
People should be made aware	26	21.7
Problem of fund should be solved	11	09.2
Committees should be given maximum powers	04	03.3
Information related to income/expenditure should be made public	03	02.5
Poor should be given more powers/Poor should be listened first	07	05.8
Women's problem should be solved	13	10.8
Information given should be made compulsory	05	04.2
Gram Sabha should be empowered with more powers	11	09.2
People should be educated	08	06.7
Sarpanch should be given more power	03	02.5
Sarpanch's power should be curtailed	03	02.5
Everybody should come in Gram Sabha	03	02.5
No Suggestions	42	35.0

Thus, it is clear from the above analysis that almost two-thirds respondents have suggestions to improve the Gram Swaraj system, which is very significant in many respects. Awareness generation and educating people have come out as significant suggestions, whereas other important suggestions have also come out.

To conclude, it can be inferred that all the three categories SC, OBC and general in the selected village population are properly represented in the sample. Majority group of respondents is below the age of 40. Since one-third representation of female is made mandatory for the quorum of Gram Sabha meeting, it substantiates the fact that the sample is also represented by almost one-third female. Almost three-fourths of the respondents are educated up to various levels. Looking into the rural background of respondents and also one-third female, it appears that the educational level is considerably very good. Majority of the respondents do agriculture work. A significant number of respondents are housewife.

About two-thirds respondents are aware about this very important aspect of Panchayat Raj that at the grassroots level the Gram Sabha has been specially empowered. It is indeed a matter of big satisfaction that overwhelming majority of the respondents point out regularity of Gram Sabha meetings. It is interesting to note that almost three-fourths of the respondents know the required number of quorum. The percentage is lower who know the required women presence as compared to those who know the quorum required for Gram Sabha meetings. Though, the number of respondents is slightly lower who know the required number of women for quorum, nevertheless it is a positive indication that this significant aspect of mandatory women participation is known by a considerable number. Almost two-thirds respondents know that SCs/STs presence in Gram Sabha is necessary.

A significant percentage of respondents are not participating in the Gram Sabha meetings. On the contrary majority of the respondents are aware of the facts like, required number of quorum for Gram Sabha meeting and mandatory presence of women and SCs/STs. The major reasons for non-participation shown by the respondents are their extraordinary busy schedule, not getting information and social taboos. Three-fourths of the respondents get the information of Gram Sabha through the chowkidar who is assigned for this task. It is indeed a positive indicator that more than 85 per cent respondents get the information of Gram Sabha. A limited number of respondents get this information in the prescribed time, nevertheless overwhelming majority of respondents get the information of the meeting, since the village society is very close and informal and therefore it is believed that this information can be given as per the convenience of the villagers and chowkidar. A significant percentage do not know the number of Gram Sabha meetings held in the last one year. Nevertheless, the number of meetings held is known by more than half of the respondents.

More than one-third respondents do not know the level of presence of any group in Gram Sabha. A small group of respondents feel that SCs, higher groups and educated groups present almost all in the meetings. Except female the presence of almost half of all groups in the meeting is pointed out by one-third to half of the respondents. Female group is cited maximum in the categories of very few and do not come to participate in the meetings. Educated and higher group discuss the issue in Gram Sabha. SCs, women and weaker sections sit silently, whereas women make only signatures in meetings. And also majority of the respondents do not know the level of participation of different groups. In majority cases the reason of non-participation is due to personal reasons and exceptionally in female it is due to social evils.

Local problem is the main issue of discussion in meetings. It is indeed an issue of concern that a significant number is not aware about the issues of discussion. Nevertheless, looking into the rural exposure to the issue, it is a positive indication. A sizeable number of respondents have expressed their views that the decisions are unanimous in Gram Sabha meetings. At the same time almost equal number of respondents do not know about decision-making but even than it confirms that slowly and gradually people are getting closer to the issues of panchayats. Though, the number is limited who have raised the issues in Gram Sabha meeting but the issues raised are mainly related to infrastructure and construction work, which is significant from the point of view of overall development of villages.

Majority of the respondents do not raise the issue in Gram Sabha since they do not go to meetings, whereas a significant number do not require it. It is a positive indication that almost half of the respondents are of the view that the decisions are unanimous. Influential people and Sarpanch continue to influence the decision-making process in Gram Sabha meeting.

All significant problems were identified and in all cases the respondents were clear about their views. Only one or two respondents gave the response of do not know. Electricity, drainage and employment are considered as big problems by majority respondents. The number of respondents is very limited who have raised any problem in the Gram Sabha meetings. On the contrary, majority respondents know the prevailing problems at the village level. In fact, if any issue is raised in Gram Sabha meeting, the issue has to be discussed threadbare and then some appropriate proposal is to be forwarded to the concerned agencies. It is therefore very obvious to get such responses to the problem.

It is a positive indication that in majority respondents' point of view, the listed 15 works either done one-two times or regularly by panchayats, whereas a considerable number do not know. Looking into the village clientele's exposure and understanding, it is indeed a step forward that people are taking a gripe over the functional issues of panchayat.

Majority respondents do not know the committee system. Most of the respondents who are aware about the committees know about the various committees' formation. Still a major chunk of the respondent does not know about the specific works of specific committees. Nevertheless a sizeable number has given specific works, which is of significant importance from the point of view of Gram Swaraj system. Majority respondents are not familiar with the committee formation procedure. Nevertheless one-third respondents provide the right procedure of formation, which is a positive indication. Almost half of the selected members are members in various committees. It shows that through committee system maximum villagers are directly associated with the implementation of Gram Swaraj. The selected respondents represent almost all committees. A small number is not aware about the name of the specific committee regarding their membership. Maximum respondents are favouring unanimous decision-making with mutual consent in committees. Almost one-fourth do not know about this. Looking into the innovation and its technicality a sizeable number is coming closer to understand the system.

The village level individuals are known to maximum respondents whereas the Janpad and district level officials are also known to almost one-third respondents. The lowest known individual is stakeholder. It is due to the matter of the fact that firstly it is a new concept emerged out with Gram Swaraj and secondly people are not well versed with this inclusion of stakeholder in the various committees.

One very important aspect of Gram Swaraj, Gram Kosh is not seriously taken into consideration. The obvious reason for such poor response is lack of information regarding Gram Kosh and its functioning utility among villagers. A very limited number know the Gram Kosh and out of them a small number know the various koshas under Gram Kosh. Majority respondents' opinion is in favour of unanimous election of Koshadhyaksha.

Various facts of last work done by the panchayat are known to one-fourth or below percentage of respondents. Looking in the technicality of the issue, it is a welcome sign. Almost one-third respondents have witnessed the positive change in the role of Sarpanch whereas more than half of the respondents find no difference in the role. An overwhelming majority of the respondents cite cooperative attitude of rural elite, which has special meaning from the point of view of rural socio-economic disparities and hegemonic situations of a few.

Three-fourth of the respondents find PR representatives and officials attitude good and cooperative which is really very important for the smooth functioning of the Gram Sabha. Almost half of the respondents do not find any change due to Gram Swaraj whereas more than a third respondents see positive change.

Significant number could provide the positive difference in the system after Gram Swaraj, at the same time a remarkable number do not find any difference. In fact it is all because at the grassroots level people are not made aware of the system.

One-third respondents are recognising the role of weaker section as decisive. It is quite obvious that the amendment package has many special dimensions for the participation of weaker sections but since this new phenomenon has not yet been properly disseminated to the masses, in such circumstances the percentage saying 'yes' is very encouraging. It is indeed significant that weaker section has active participation in process.

In fact, due to lack of exposure and understanding of the Gram Swaraj the number of persons acquainted with the problem are very limited but nevertheless a limited number of respondents has cited all possible problems in the smooth functioning of Gram Swaraj. Almost two-third respondents have made suggestions to improve the Gram Swaraj system, which is very significant in many respects. Awareness generation and educating people have come out as significant suggestions whereas other important suggestions are also of significance to improve the grassroots situation.

7

Conclusion

Panchayat Raj, as a system of governance at the grassroots level in rural India, has rightly been conceived as the most viable and proper mechanism of realising the goals of democracy and decentralisation. After Independence, efforts have been made to create the units of self-governance at grassroots level but all in vain since they could not produce the desired results. During the Gandhian era and afterward a debate was going on for the strengthening of Panchayat Raj Institutions (PRIs) at local level and Central Government's initiative came out with 73rd Amendment for PRIs in India.

The 73rd Amendment to the Constitution of India not only gives a constitutional status to the panchayats; it also provides uniformity and formal structure to these traditional institutions of self-governance for the sake of their effective functioning. The earlier attempts at institutionalising the panchayats were half-hearted and failed due to the absence of supportive constitutional measures and lack of political will. The 73rd Amendment initiates, a fundamental restructuring of governance and administrative system of the country, based on the philosophy of decentralisation and power to the people. The pioneering and innovative initiatives of Madhya Pradesh government in strengthening and institutionalising decentralised rural self-governance in the post-73rd Amendment phase generated immense interest among the observers and experts, who were keen to understand this significant change in the pattern of governance at the grassroots level.

In the continuation of the process of strengthening decentralised governance at local level, an innovation of Gram Swaraj system was introduced on 26 January, 2001. In this context, it becomes imperative to go beyond the government's stated objectives, rules and regulations, Acts and claims of effective functioning of Gram Swaraj, and take an objective look at the ground reality and also to understand and analyse the innovations made by the State Government through Gram Swaraj.

This study is an attempt to identify, document and comprehend the broad trends emanating from the field, based on the experience of three years' functioning of Gram Swaraj in Madhya Pradesh. Three years is a short span of time for the dust to settle from such radical changes. However, it is important to understand and analyse the process and direction of institutionalisation of the present system and its status in the initial phase (2001 to 2004), which would have a significant impact and critical lessons for charting out the future course of action for effective people-centric development and governance not only in the state but across the country.

II

In Madhya Pradesh, efforts have been made by enacting laws that further the cause of decentralised governance. The Madhya Pradesh Panchayat Act, 1962, was one such effort based on the recommendations of the Balwant Rai Mehta Committee. A new Panchayat Raj Act was enacted in 1981, which was later amended in 1988 to provide reservations of seats for SCs, STs and women in panchayats. Elections to these bodies were not held regularly and the bodies remained under the control of government-appointed administrators. The Madhya Pradesh Panchayat Raj Act, 1990, attempted to revitalise the PRIs and transfer power to the people to ensure their effective participation. The key features of this Act were direct elections to these bodies, involvement of political parties, and the transfer of resources and developmental machinery to the panchayats.

The Madhya Pradesh Panchayat Raj Act, 1993, was enacted to cover the lacunae in existing laws for the establishment of panchayat institutions. This Act was drafted in conformity with the objectives, substance and directives of the 73rd Constitutional Amendment Act.

Panchayat Raj system in Madhya Pradesh has not remained static but evolved in the last ten years. A dynamic and adaptive Panchayat Raj system has ensured the success of PRIs in the State. This adaptiveness is reflected in the various Amendments made to the Panchayat Raj Act, 1993, and the ever-evolving office orders issued to operationalise and institutionalise the Panchayat Raj system.

Several challenges to the Panchayat Raj system have emerged during the last ten years of its operationalisation in Madhya Pradesh. Fortunately, a proactive State Government has responded to these needs and challenges. The government analysed the strain on the system and identified the problem areas, and made a serious attempt to address these problem areas at all levels. The causative factors were identified in the underlying panchayat laws and the Panchayat Raj system as enunciated in the Madhya Pradesh Panchayat Raj Act, 1993. The State Government, in earnest to resolve these constraints, changed and reissued its office orders, and also amended the Panchayat Act itself. This willingness and flexibility of the State Government to tackle bottlenecks has given strength to the Panchayat Raj system in Madhya Pradesh. It also reflects the political will to ensure the success of Panchayat Raj system in the state. The amendments have given much-needed elasticity to the system and have contributed to the success of the Panchayat Raj system in Madhya Pradesh as institutions of grass-roots democracy. A dynamic system where information flows upward from the bottom, and a system that responds and adjusts to these stimuli, is a truly democratic and representative system. The

State Government has made more than ten amendments to the Madhya Pradesh Panchayat Act, 1993. Drawing on experience gathered in the functioning of the PRIs, the State Government has amended the Panchayat Act to genuinely strengthen and empower the Panchayat Raj system.

An analysis of the amendments clearly reflects the government's desire to institutionalise and empower the system. The amendments deal with the teething problems of the system. Via the amendments, the State Government has tried to overcome limitations that had cropped up during implementation of the Act.

The aim, in addition to strengthening the panchayat, is also to articulate and define the functional space of these institutions. A constant endeavour was to define the function of these institutions and devolve more administrative and financial powers to the panchayats. Simultaneously, the amendments try to guarantee socio-economic change in favour of the marginalised, as envisaged in the 73rd Constitutional Amendment. The State Government, through the Amendments, has tried to operationalise the panchayats, consistent with the ideology of 'power to people' and democratic decentralisation. The amendments made in the Panchayat Act in 2001 paved the way for the introduction of Gram Swaraj.

III

This study is an attempt to document the processes of change in Madhya Pradesh, which led to the establishment of Gram Swaraj, and also to fully comprehend and analyse the implications of the making as the pivot of grassroots democracy.

The main focus of this research is the Gram Sabha within the Panchayat Raj system. The panchayat representatives, native elites, local bureaucracy and Gram Sabha members have been considered within the study, so as to comprehend the dynamics of its working, change and development. The study also seeks to understand the interplay, interlinkages and conflict between these actors. Study focuses on the conditions for the implementation of Gram Swaraj and its implications on the PRIs in particular and governance space in Madhya Pradesh in general.

The major concern of the research is to study the experiment of Gram Swaraj in Madhya Pradesh. Two districts of the state are selected purposively for the micro-level study. The selected districts are Shajapur and Dewas. A proportionate sampling framework has been adopted. For a proper special coverage one block was selected from each selected district. From the selected blocks, five Gram Panchayats were selected where due representation was given to women-headed Gram Panchayats. Gram Sabha members, committee chairpersons/members and panchayat representatives were the units of observation. From each selected Gram Panchayat – six Gram Sabha members, (three male and three female), five standing committee chairpersons/members, five panchayat representatives (one Sarpanch, one Up-sarpanch and three Panch), one Koshadhyaksha and one Panchayat Secretary were taken for an interview. In all, from two blocks of two districts the size of sample was 60 Gram Sabha Members, 120 standing committee chairpersons/members, panchayat representatives, Koshadhyaksha and Panchayat Secretary. The total size of sample was 180. The study is mainly based on primary data. On the basis of collected data, a code book was prepared. All the interview schedules were coded accordingly. Coded schedules were entered in the computer. SPSS (version 10) package was used for analysis and interpretation of data.

IV

Present study is based on primary data. For the purpose of data collection and to understand the grassroots reality, 10 villages were selected for an in-depth survey. Two separate interview schedules were administered for Panchayat Raj representatives and Gram Sabha members respectively. Besides these, a village listing schedule and a questionnaire were also administered to know the profile of the villages, meetings of Gram Sabhas, participation of people and other similar issues.

The households represented in panchayats vary from village to village. However, the average representation ratio is high and if the rotatory system of representation allows maximum households to represent the panchayat, the system would throw up a seasoned, experienced and informed lot of members in village. Since the required quorum for the Gram Sabha meeting is one-fifth of the total member, the requisite number is maintained with great difficulty; in fact a very minuscule number in every village attends the meetings regularly while a considerably high number never attends meetings. It is surprising to note that this apathy of the villagers, particularly when the panchayats have been given most of the powers to make them units of self-governance

In majority cases nobody attends the meeting, whereas a significant number opine that only men attend the meetings. Despite having a statutory provision of one-third representation of women for the quorum of Gram Sabha meeting, a clear-cut apathy is discernible among the households.

V

This part concludes the attitudes and perceptions of the Panchayat Raj representatives – the operators of the system.

To conclude, it can be inferred that all the categories in the selected village population are properly represented in the sample. The majority group of respondents is below the age of 50. The representation of male and female is in four-one ratio. Majority of respondents are educated up to various levels. Educational level of respondents is considerably very good. Majority of the respondents do agriculture work and a significant number of respondents are housewives.

Three-fourths of respondents are of the view that their candidature for panchayat was decided by villagers. It is indeed a positive indication for democracy at local level. It is also a matter of satisfaction that by election two-thirds respondents have come in panchayat whereas one-third entered in panchayat unopposed. In majority cases the respondents do not have any previous experience of the working in panchayat.

It is interesting to note that overwhelming majority of the respondents feel that meetings are regular. The respondents have pointed out some specific reasons for non-regularity of panchayat meetings. It is a positive indication that almost three-fourths of the respondents attend the meetings regularly. Respondents have pointed out lack of timely information and personal work as the major reasons for not attending the meetings of panchayat. Majority of the respondents discuss issues in panchayat meetings. Almost one-fourth respondents play an idle role, nevertheless the positive majority opinion matters with respect to functioning.

Half of the respondents visit Tehsil and Janpad Panchayat. A considerable number of them visit Zilla Panchayat. Remaining offices are visited by a limited number. The exposure of respondents clearly demonstrates that the Sarpanch, secretary and some other representatives visit the offices for panchayat work. The visits are mostly done for the sake of solving village problem, panchayat work or official work. Though the number is limited but it is important that they are well versed with the functional and operational aspect of panchayat.

MLA is the most known person to the respondents. Chairperson of Zilla and Janpad Panchayat and Minister in-charge are also known by a significant number of respondents. Since these persons are directly involved in helping panchayats for various works, the local leadership is more exposed about them. Collector, once the most powerful district official, is the least known name to local leadership now.

It is indeed a matter of concern that almost half of respondents have made efforts for doing some work in panchayat and that too when among the respondents very few are Sarpanch and remaining are panch. It is very encouraging and positive sign that in majority opinion the selection of beneficiaries is done as per the rules. Though one-fourth respondents still feel that Sarpanch/secretary fulfil this job.

It is indeed a matter of big satisfaction that overwhelming majority of the respondents point out regularity of Gram Sabha meetings, which is of very significance from the point of view of success of Gram Swaraj system in Madhya Pradesh. It is interesting to note that almost two-thirds of the respondents know this factual information. An overwhelming percentage of respondents is well aware of the women presence required for quorum of Gram Sabha meetings. It is a positive indication that this significant aspect of mandatory women participation is known by a considerable number. A significant percentage of respondents are regularly participating in the meetings. Only a very small number never participated in the meetings. Major reasons shown by the respondents for not attending the meetings are their extraordinary busy schedule, not getting information and nobody listens.

Training has not been adequately carried out to make the panchayat representatives aware about the procedural aspect of Gram Swaraj. The respondents have mainly received the training from district or block headquarters. It is clear from the analysis that the respondents have mainly received basic clarity about Gram Swaraj through training. Local problem is the main issue of discussion in meetings. Almost three-fourths respondents have expressed their views that the decisions are unanimous. It confirms that slowly and gradually people are getting closer to the issues of panchayats.

It is a positive indication that three-fourths respondents are contacted by the villagers for panchayat related work. The respondents have pointed out reason of meetings to share village problem or personal problem. In most of the cases either the problems are decreased after Gram Swaraj or remained same. Exceptionally, the health problem is referred as increased.

After discussing all the solutions for different problems before and after Gram Swaraj, it is clear that the solution procedure remained more or less same. It can be so because, firstly the new system has spent a very little span of time and secondly, the issues are of the nature that they cannot be solved within the given situation and resources.

In majority cases there is no meeting with important individuals. It is obvious because in sample we have selected Up-sarpanch and Panch as well, and usually the meetings with important individuals is done by Sarpanch. Even then a considerable number has contacted all important individuals many times. It clearly confirms that the local leadership is contacting all the important individuals for panchayat work.

Almost two-thirds respondents feel that nobody dominated Panchayat/Gram Sabha. It is indeed a positive and encouraging sign that usually respondents do not observe that there is any domination. Though Sarpanch and anti-social elements are also referred as dominant groups; that is a real cause for worry for the Panchayat/Gram Sabha.

Overwhelming majority of the respondents make their point that they never find any issue as a bone of contention in Panchayat/Gram Sabha. It is definitely a matter of big satisfaction that Panchayat/Gram Sabha are not the platforms where disputes are raised and discussed.

People having village development attitude, educated people and local leaders are considered good for better performance in panchayat. It demonstrates that at local level, conceptually the respondents agree to have better leadership.

It is a positive indication that in majority cases school, anganwadi, welfare schemes, construction work and development work are inspected. Usually, these are prominent works at grassroots level. Since streetlight and water supply are not provided by panchayats in many cases and therefore they do not have any role to inspect such activities.

Almost half of the respondents know the Gram Kosh and out of them a considerable number know the various koshas under Gram Kosh. Majority respondents' opinion is in favour of unanimous election of Koshadhyaksha. A considerable number is well versed with all the steps for the completion of a work along with the details of each activity. This awareness is a good depiction of healthy scenario for the better and transparent functioning of panchayats.

The selected respondents represent various committees but are small in number, whereas majority respondents are not members of any committee. Less than half of the respondents point out that meetings are held. It is definitely a new innovation and through committees, specific issues are to be discussed but people are not made properly aware about the committee system and therefore the committee meetings are not taking place in majority cases. In committee meetings, all major issues related to village are discussed in committee meetings.

The opinion about Gram Swaraj is of a mixed nature but the positive opinion is out weighting the negative that has a significant meaning for the system of Gram Swaraj. Due to Gram Swaraj caste differentiation has decreased from the point of view of majority respondents. Though there are views that there is no difference or casteism has increased but nevertheless in majority opinion caste differentiation is decreased due to Gram Swaraj.

Significant number of respondents believe that the due procedure is adopted whereas almost one-fourth of the respondents do not find any change. Since fingers have been raised on the selection procedure of beneficiaries prior to Gram Swaraj it is indeed a positive feedback that in majority opinion the selection is adhered to with due procedure.

Only few changes are suggested by a small number of respondents whereas a sizeable number advocate for no change. It promotes the credibility of the new system. An overwhelming majority of the respondents feel no change in the attitude of socio-economic elite. It is indeed a matter of concern from the point of view of village society and smooth functioning of Gram Sabha, it is urgently needed to sensitise the village society for the socio-economic equity and awareness for equal opportunities of occasions for everyone.

In fact, due to lack of exposure and understanding of the Gram Swaraj the number of persons acquainted with the problem are very limited and also a considerable number either do not know any problem or do not find any problems nevertheless all the possible problems are cited by respondents.

Almost half of the respondents have suggestions to improve the Gram Swaraj system, which is very significant in many respects. Awareness generation and educating people have come out as significant suggestions whereas other important suggestions have also come out.

VI

This part concludes the attitudes and perceptions of the Gram Sabha members. To conclude, it can be inferred that all the three categories – SC, OBC and general – in the selected village population are properly represented in the sample. Majority group of respondents is below the age of 40. Since one-third representation of female is made mandatory for the quorum of Gram Sabha meeting, it substantiates the fact that the sample is also represented by almost one-third female. Almost three-fourths of the respondents are educated up to various levels. Looking into the rural background of respondents and also one-third female, it appears that the educational level is considerably very good. Majority of the respondents do agriculture work. A significant number of respondents are housewife.

About two-thirds respondents are aware about this very important aspect of Panchayat Raj that at the grassroots level the Gram Sabha has been specially empowered. It is indeed a matter of big satisfaction that overwhelming majority of the respondents point out regularity of Gram Sabha meetings. It is interesting to note that almost three-fourths of the respondents know the required number of quorum. The percentage is lower who know the required women's presence as compared to those who know the quorum required for Gram Sabha meetings. Though, the number of respondents is slightly lower who know the required number of women for quorum, nevertheless it is a positive indication that this significant aspect of mandatory women's participation is known by a considerable number. Almost two-thirds respondents know that SCs/STs presence in Gram Sabha is necessary.

A significant percentage of respondents are not participating in the Gram Sabha meetings. On the contrary majority of the respondents are aware of the facts like required number of quorum for Gram Sabha meeting and mandatory presence of women and

SCs/STs. The major reasons for non-participation shown by the respondents are their extraordinary busy schedule, not getting information and social taboos. Three-fourths of the respondents get the information of Gram Sabha through the chowkidar who is assigned for this task. It is indeed a positive indicator that more than 85 per cent respondents get the information of Gram Sabha. A limited number of respondents get this information in the prescribed time, nevertheless overwhelming majority of the respondents get the information of the meeting. Since the village society is very close and informal and therefore it is believed that this information can be given as per the convenience of the villagers and chowkidar. A significant percentage does not know the number of Gram Sabha meetings held in last one year. Nevertheless the number of meetings held is known by more than half of the respondents.

More than one-third respondents do not know the level of presence of any group in Gram Sabha. A small group of respondents feel that SCs, higher groups and educated groups present almost all in the meetings. Except female the presence of almost half of all groups in the meeting is pointed out by one-third to half of the respondents. Female group is cited maximum in the categories of very few and do not come to participate in the meetings. Educated and higher group discuss the issues in Gram Sabha. SCs, women and weaker sections sit silently, whereas women make only signatures in meetings. And also majority of the respondents do not know the level of participation of different groups. In majority cases the reason of non-participation is due to personal reasons and exceptionally in females it is due to social evils.

Local problem is the main issue of discussion in meetings. It is indeed an issue of concern that a significant number is not aware about the issues of discussion. Nevertheless, looking into the rural exposure to the issue, it is a positive indication. A sizeable number of respondents have expressed their views that the decisions are unanimous in Gram Sabha meetings. At the same time almost equal number of respondents do not know about decision-making but even then it confirms that slowly and gradually people are getting closer to the issues of panchayats. Though, the number is limited who have raised the issues in Gram Sabha meetings but the issues raised are mainly related to infrastructure and construction work, which is significant from the point of view of overall development of villages.

Majority of the respondents do not raise the issue in Gram Sabha since they do not go to meetings, whereas a significant number do not require it. It is a positive indication that almost half of the respondents are of the view that the decisions are unanimous. Influential people and Sarpanch continue to influence the decision-making process in Gram Sabha meeting.

All significant problems were identified and in all cases the respondents were clear about their views. Only one or two respondents gave the response of do not know. Electricity, drainage and employment are considered as big problems by majority respondents. The number of respondents who have raised any problem in the Gram Sabha meetings is very limited. On the contrary, majority respondents know the prevailing problems at the village level. In fact, if any issue is raised in Gram Sabha meeting, the issue has to be discussed threadbare and then some appropriate proposal is to be forwarded to the concerned agencies. It is therefore very obvious to get such responses to the problem.

It is a positive indication that in majority respondent's point of view the listed 15 works either done one-two times or regularly by panchayats, whereas a considerable number do not know. Looking into the village clientele's exposure and understanding, it is indeed a step forward that people are taking a grip over the functional issues of panchayat.

Majority respondents do not know the committee system. Most of the respondents who are aware about the committees know about the various committees' formation. Still a major chunk of the respondent does not know about the specific works of specific committees. Nevertheless, a sizeable number has given specific works, which is of significant importance from the point of view of Gram Swaraj system. Majority respondents are not familiar with the committee formation procedure. Nevertheless one-third respondents provide the right procedure of formation, which is a positive indication. Almost half of the selected members are members in various committees. It shows that through committee system, maximum villagers are directly associated with the implementation of Gram Swaraj. The selected respondents represent almost all committees. A small number is not aware about the name of the specific committee regarding their membership. Maximum respondents are favouring unanimous decision-making with mutual consent in committees. Almost one-fourth do not know about this. Looking into the innovation and its technicality a sizeable number is coming closer to understanding the system.

Maximum respondents know the village level individuals, whereas the Janpad and district level officials are also known to almost one-third respondents. The lowest known individual is the stakeholder. It is due to the fact that first, it is a new concept emerged out with Gram Swaraj and second people are not well versed with this inclusion of stakeholder in the various committees.

One very important aspect of Gram Swaraj, Gram Kosh is not seriously taken into consideration. The obvious reason for such poor response is lack of information regarding Gram Kosh and its functioning utility among villagers. A very limited number know the Gram Kosh and out of them a small number know the various koshas under Gram Kosh. Majority respondents' opinion is in favour of unanimous election of Koshadhyaksha.

Various facts of last work done by the panchayat are known to one-fourth or below percentage of respondents. Looking in the technicality of the issue, it is a welcome sign. Almost one-third respondents have witnessed the positive change in the role of Sarpanch, whereas more than half of the respondents find no difference in the role. An overwhelming majority of the respondents cite cooperative attitude of rural elite, which has special meaning from the point of view of rural socio-economic disparities and hegemonic situations of a few.

Three-fourths of the respondents find panchayat representatives and officials' attitude good and cooperative, which is really very important for the smooth functioning of the Gram Sabha. Almost half of the respondents do not find any change due to Gram Swaraj whereas more than one-third respondents see positive change.

Significant number could provide the positive difference in the system after Gram Swaraj, at the same time a remarkable number do not find any difference. In fact it is all because at the grassroots level people are not made aware of the system.

One-third respondents are recognising the role of weaker section, decisive. It is quite obvious that the amendment package has many special dimensions for the participation of weaker section but since this new phenomenon has not yet been properly disseminated to the masses, in such a circumstances the percentage saying 'yes' is very encouraging. It is indeed significant that weaker section has active participation in the process.

In fact, due to lack of exposure and understanding of the Gram Swaraj the number of persons acquainted with the problem are very limited but nevertheless a limited number of respondents has cited all possible problems in the smooth functioning of Gram Swaraj. Almost two-thirds respondents have made suggestions to improve the Gram Swaraj system, which is very significant in many respects. Awareness generation and educating people have come out as significant suggestions, whereas other important suggestions are also of significance to improve the grassroots situation.

VII

It has been evident from the working experience of Gram Swaraj and also as the above mentioned responses of respondents indicate that the level of participation of people at grassroots level has been relatively low. Despite knowing the procedural aspect, Gram Sabhas are almost a formal institution. The State Government transferred nearly all of the powers previously exercised by Gram Panchayats to Gram Sabha. It has thus gone from representative democracy at the grassroots to direct democracy but the fact remains that despite this endeavour there is a clear cut gap between macro-level decisions and grassroots reality.

The grassroots experiences suggest that majority of the panchayat representatives and villagers are aware about the procedural aspects of Gram Sabha meetings. Gram Sabhas are provided supreme position in the new system but people at large are least informed about these provisions. They still accept the supremacy of Gram Panchayat.

It seems that only amendment in the State Act and specific provisions for new system will not change the scenario. There is an urgent need to opt for an effective device, whereby maximum people can be informed, made aware and motivated to come forward for the proper implementation and execution of Gram Swaraj. There is an urgent need to break the culture of silence and to strive for capacity building, sensitisation and orientation to improve the grassroots scenario.

Suggestions

1. The Panchayat Raj Institutions (PRIs) through Gram Swaraj have specially empowered people to work as units of self-governance but it has been observed that the level of awareness and exposure among Panchayat Raj representatives and Gram Sabha members are very low. It is therefore important to initiate special training packages, awareness campaigns and capacity building programmes.
2. It appears that the required number for quorum is very high, which needs to be relooked with ground reality.
3. The provisions of the State Acts should be translated into simple Hindi and local dialect and be distributed to all panchayat functionaries in the form of pocket booklets as ready reckoners. Posters can also be prepared and displayed on the walls of Gram Panchayat building.
4. It has often been seen that the Gram Sabha members find it difficult to perform their duties due to the complicated rules and procedures. It is, therefore necessary that the rules and procedure be simplified and included in the pocket booklets.
5. Committee system in Gram Swaraj is a special feature to tackle the issue of multifaceted and overall development of

the village but the rural people are not well versed with the specificity of such system, therefore it is needed to make the people and members of the committees informed about the dynamics of committee system at length.

6. Gram Sabhas have been provided supreme position in the new system but people at large are least informed about these provisions. They are still accepting the supremacy of Gram Panchayat. It is important to make them aware about such provisions. For this purpose public awareness campaigns can be launched through NGOs. Electronic media (Community Television) can also be an effective medium.
7. The list of assigned works to Gram Sabha includes multi-faceted task including management of natural resources (including land, water and forest). This provision can provide ample opportunities to rural masses for better living conditions and livelihood bases. It is suggested that the activities of watershed and other similar activities should be taken up by Gram Sabhas in their respective areas on voluntary basis. People's participation can change the scenario drastically. The need is orientation of people for such works.
8. Gram Sabha has to perform a very specific role to tackle social issue as well. Here is a significant aspect that the Gram Sabhas should also take lead to minimise the social evils. Use of liquor and practice of dowry are to be discouraged.
9. Rural regions are facing chronic drought, which leads to acute shortage of food, starvation and compulsion of migration. It is therefore important to prepare panchayats with all such training and awareness campaigns to face such natural disasters. Better management skills can reduce the intensity of disasters.
10. The study suggests that merely by resorting to amendment in the State Act and specific provisions for new system cannot change the scenario of villages. There is an urgent need to explore effective devices whereby maximum people can be informed, made aware and motivated to come forward for the proper implementation and execution of Gram Swaraj.

Participation in Gram Sabha meetings has been low despite knowing the Gram Swaraj. Low participation can be mainly attributed to the strong and invincible caste, class and gender divide in villages. Sarpanch and other influential people dominate in decision-making process. There are two prominent and sharply contrasting groups leading the panchayats – the group of traditionally influential representatives and the other of new entrants. The idea of participation as an important part of Panchayat Raj has not been observed in practice. In fact, in retrospect, it seems inevitable that persons of influence would look at larger community participation with hostility. The vibrancy and efficacy of Gram Sabha will remain dismal if it does not possess the capacity to perform assigned roles and responsibility. This question becomes more pertinent in a socio-cultural milieu where human resource development is low and society is deeply fragmented and hierarchical. And therefore it is urgently needed that marginalised sections of society which have been out from the process of decision-making have to be taken into the mainstream through sensitisation and capacity building. The experience suggests that the resource flow, Gram Sabha and its ever-increasing powers and authority has generated a lot of interest in people. It is expected that this interest is likely to be translated into a more broad based and participative leadership at grassroots level. The need is to address the issue of awareness generation among masses. Training camps, awareness campaigns and audio-visual mediums can be of critical importance for sensitisation and capacity building.

Bibliography

Ambedkar, B.R. (1948): Speech in the Constituent Assembly on 4 November 1948, in Vasant Moon (ed.) (1994) *Writing and Speeches*, 13: 61-61. Education Department, Government of Maharashtra, Mumbai.

Aziz, Abdul (1993): *Decentralised Planning: The Karnataka Experiment*, Sage Publications, New Delhi.

Bajpai, Ashok and Verma, M.S. (1995): *Panchayati Raj in India: A New Thrust*, Vol. 1, Sahitya Prakashan, New Delhi.

Bandyopadhyay, D. and Mukherjee, Amitabh (2004): *New Issues in Panchayati Raj*, Concept Publishing Company, New Delhi.

Behar, Amitabh and Kumar, Yogesh (2002): "Decentralisation in Madhya Pradesh, India: from Panchayati Raj to Gram Swaraj (1995 to 2001)", *Working Paper 170*, ODI, London, UK.

Bhadouria, B.P.S. (ed.) (1988): *Decentralised Planning for Development in India*, Commonwealth Publishers, New Delhi.

Bhargava, B.S. and Subha, K. (1995): *Emerging Trends in Panchayati Raj in India*, NIRD and Konrad Adenauer Stiftung.

Bhat, UKS (1995): *New Panchayati Raj System*, Printwell, Jaipur.

Chakrabortty, K. and Bhattacharyya, S.K. (1993): *Leadership Factions and Panchayati Raj: A Case Study of West Bengal*, Rawat Publications, Jaipur.

Choudhary, R.C. and Jain S.P. (1999): *Strengthening Village Democracy*, National Institute of Rural Development, Hyderabad.

Datta, Prabhat Kumar (1996): "Rural Development through Panchayats: The West Bengal Experiences", *Kurukshetra*, 44(7): 65, April.

Datta, Prabhat (1995): "Village self-government in Post-colonial India", *Kurukshetra*, 43(7): 52, April.

Desai, Vasant (1990): *Panchayati Raj: Power to the People*, Himalaya Publishing House, Bombay.

Dikshit, G.S. (1964): *Local Self-Government in Medieval Karnataka*, Karnataka University, Dharwad.

Dutta, Prabhat (1993): *Second Generation Panchayats in India*, Calcutta Book House Pvt. Ltd., Calcutta.

Dwivedi, R.S. (2000): *Madhya Pradesh Panchayat Raj Adhiniyam*, Suvidha Law House, Bhopal.

Fernandes, A. (1999): "Reconnecting the Sabha to Gram", paper presented at the National Conference on Gram Sabha, National Institute of Rural Development, Hyderabad, July 28-29.

Gandhi, M.K. (1989) *Panchayati Raj*, Navjivan Publishing House, Ahmedabad.

Institute of Social Sciences (1994): *Decentralised Planning and Panchayati Raj*, Concept Publishing Company, New Delhi.

Institute of Social Studies (1995): *Status of Panchayati Raj in the States of India 1994,* Concept Book Publishers, New Delhi.

Jha, S.N. and Mathur P.C. (eds.) (1999): *Decentralisation of Local Politics: Readings in Indian Government and Politics*, Sage Publications, New Delhi.

Joshi, R.P. (ed.). (1998): *Constitutionalisation of Panchayati Raj – A Reassessment*, Rawat Publications, Jaipur.

Joshi R.P. and Narwani G.S. (2002): *Panchayat Raj in India: Emerging Trends Across States*, Rawat Publications, Jaipur.

Kashyap, Subhash C. (2003): *Blueprint of Political Reform*, Shipra Publications, Delhi.

Kaushik, Susheela (1996): *Panchayati Raj in Action: Challenges to Women's Role*, Friedrich Ebert Stiftung, New Delhi.

Khanna, B.S. (1994): *Panchayati Raj in India (Rural Local Self-Government)*, Deep and Deep Publication, New Delhi.

Kothari, Rajni (1998): *State Against Democracy: In Search of Human Governance*, Ajanta Publications, Delhi.

Lal, G.M.M. (1994): *Rajiv Gandhi and Panchayati Raj: Democracy and Development of the Grassroots*, Konark Publishers Pvt. Ltd., Delhi.

Lieten, G.K. (1996): *Development Devolution and Democracy: Village Discourse in West Bengal*. Sage Publications, New Delhi.

Maheshwari, S.R. (1994): *Local Government in India*, Lakshmi Narain Agarwal, Agra.

Mander, Harsh (1999): "Towards Direct Democracy: The Legal Empowerment of Gram Sabha", *Kurukshetra*, New Delhi, Vol. 48, No. 1, October.

Mani, K.K. (Comp.) (1993): *Panchayati Raj: Gram Sarkar*, Gandhi Peace Centre, Delhi.

Manor, James (2001): "Madhya Pradesh Experiments with Direct Democracy", *Economic and Political Weekly*, March 3.

Mathew, G. and Ramesh C. Nayak (1996): "Panchayats at work: what it means for the oppressed?" *Economic and Political Weekly*, July 6.

Mathew, George (1994): *Panchayati Raj: From Legislation to Movement*, Concept Publishing Company, New Delhi.

Mathur, P.C. (1991): *Political Dynamics of Panchayati Raj: The Institutional Pendulum of Devolution and Retraction, 1959-90 with Special Reference to Rajasthan*, Konark Publishers, New Delhi.

Mathur, S.N. (1997): *Nyaya Panchayats as Instruments of Justice*, Concept Publishing Company, New Delhi.

Meenakshisundaram, S.S. (1994): *Decentralisation in Developing Countries*, Concept Publishing Company, New Delhi.

Mehta, Asoka (Chairman) (1978): *Report of the Committee on Panchayati Raj Institutions*, Ministry of Agriculture and Irrigation, Department of Rural Development, Government of India, New Delhi.

Mishra, S.N. and Singh, S.S. (1993): *Roads to Model Panchayati Raj: Review of Panchayati Raj Acts in the Context of 73rd Constitutional Amendment Act*, Mittal Publications, New Delhi.

Mishra, S.N., Kumar, L. and Pal, C. (1998): *New Panchayati Raj in Action*, Mittal Publications, New Delhi.

Mukarji, Nirmal; Yugandhar, B.N.; Mukherjee, S.P. and Meenakshisundaram, S.S. (1995): *Peoples Representatives and Bureaucracy: The Interface in Panchayati Raj*, Institute of Social Sciences, New Delhi.

Nambiar, Malini (2001): "Making the Gram Sabha Work", *Economic and Political Weekly*, August 18.

Oommen, M.A. (1995): *Panchayati Raj Development Report*, Institute of Social Sciences, New Delhi.

Oommen, M.A. and Datta, A. (1995): *Panchayats and their Finance*, Institute of Social Sciences. Concept Publishing Company, New Delhi.

Palanithurai, G. (1994): *Empowering People for Prosperity: A Study in New Panchayati Raj System*, Kanishka Publishers, Delhi.

Palanithurai, G. (1996): *New Panchayati Raj System: Status and Prospects*, Kanishka Publishers, Delhi.

Participatory Research in Asia (2000) *Strengthening Local Self Governance in India, Finances of Panchayats in Madhya Pradesh*, Madhya Pradesh: Study sponsored by UNICEF, July 2000, PRIA, Delhi.

Purohit, B.R. (2002): "Panchayat Raj System in Scheduled Areas of Madhya Pradesh" in G. Palanithurai (ed.), *Dynamics of New Panchayati Raj System in India*, Vol. I, Concept Publishing Company, New Delhi.

Rajiv Gandhi Foundation (1994): *Issues for Discussion in Sub-Regional Workshops 1994-95 and other Documents: Task Force on Panchayati Raj*, Rajiv Gandhi Foundation, New Delhi.

Raphael, Jos C. (2000): *Decentralised Planning in India.* Anmol Publications, New Delhi. Kuhn, Berthold (1999) *Participatory Development in Rural India*, Radiant Publishers, New Delhi.

Shiviah, M. (1986): *Panchayati Raj: A Policy Perspective*, National Institute of Rural Development, Hyderabad.

Sisodia, Yatindra Singh (2002): "Decentralised Governance in Madhya Pradesh: Experiences of Gram Sabha in Scheduled Areas", *Economic and Political Weekly*, October 5.

Sisodia, Yatindra Singh (2002): "Panchayat Raj System in Madhya Pradesh: An Appraisal" in G. Palanithurai (ed.), *Dynamics of New Panchayati Raj System in India*, Vol. II, Concept Publishing Company, New Delhi.

Sisodia, Yatindra Singh (2005): "A Decade of Panchayat Raj System in Madhya Pradesh" in Yatindra Singh Sisodia (ed.), *Functioning of Panchayat Raj System*, Rawat Publications, Jaipur.

Vyasulu, Vinod (2003): *Panchayat, Democracy and Development*, Rawat Publications, Jaipur.

Index